ski·tours

OF SOUTHWESTERN COLORADO

Thomas Lepisto

Forest Roads, Trails, Touring Centers, and Backcountry Routes
Near
Durango, Silverton, Pagosa Springs,
Telluride, Ouray,
and Cortez

Conondrum Hot Springs
Have fun skiing page 147!

Thomas A. Lepisto

PRUETT P PUBLISHING COMPANY
Boulder, Colorado

Telluride Central Reservations
800 - 525- 3455

Library of Congress Cataloging-in-Publication Data

Lepisto, Thomas, 1950-
    Ski tours of southwestern Colorado

    Includes index.
    1. Cross-country skiing — Colorado — Guide-books.
2. Colorado — Description and travel — 1981-   —
Guide-books I. Title.
GV854.5.C6L46 1987   917.88   87-29119
ISBN 0-87108-748-0

First Edition
1 2 3 4 5 6 7 8 9

Printed in the United States of America.

All photographs courtesy of the author.

Cover by Richard M. Kohen.

Design & Typography —
    Richard M. Kohen, Shadow Canyon Graphics   Evergreen, Colorado

Table of Contents

C

To Linda
who added romance
to the adventure
of the ski tours
of
southwestern
Colorado.

Acknowledgements

This book could not have been written without the help and advice of many people who generously shared their knowledge of the southwestern Colorado backcountry. Walt Walker of the Fort Lewis College Outdoor Pursuits program deserves special mention, as do Bill Forsythe and the other members of the Trail Group from Ouray. Ken Paul contributed valuable advice about the routes on Wolf Creek Pass.

The instructors at the 1987 Silverton Avalanche School, especially Tim Lane and Dick and Betsy Armstrong, did a great job of conveying avalanche safety information. The personnel of the San Juan, Uncompahgre, and Rio Grande National Forests were very helpful; though providing information to the public is a routine part of their jobs, they made the extra effort to do it well. Bob Wright of the Stoner Lodge, Leith and Ruedi Bear of Bear Ranch, and Chris and Donna George of the St. Paul Ski Lodge provided information on their lodges.

My skiing companions, who were pressed into service as models for photography, have my thanks. First and foremost is my wife, Linda Faldetta, and also: Fran and Dave Hart, Jim Harvey and Joan Green, Kristi Nichols, Brenda Bailey, Lewis McCool, Steve Bortz, and Glenn McGeoch. Thanks also to Bill Dunkelberger of the Telluride Nordic Center and Dan Park of the Pagosa Pines Touring Center.

○

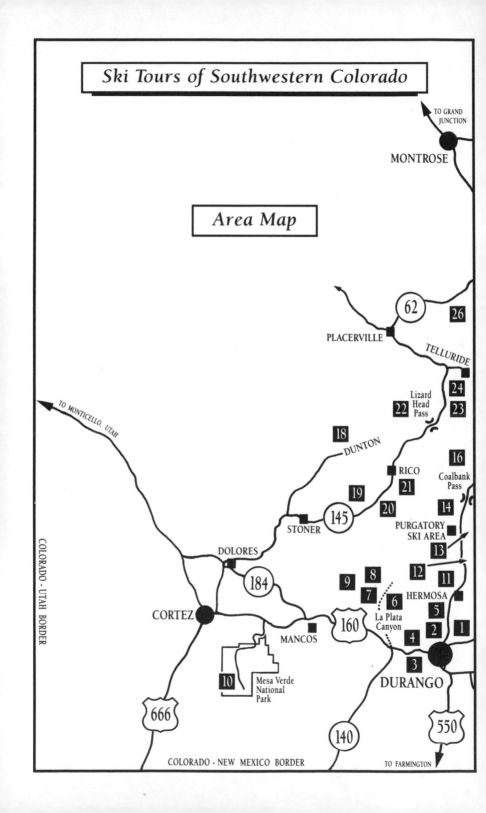

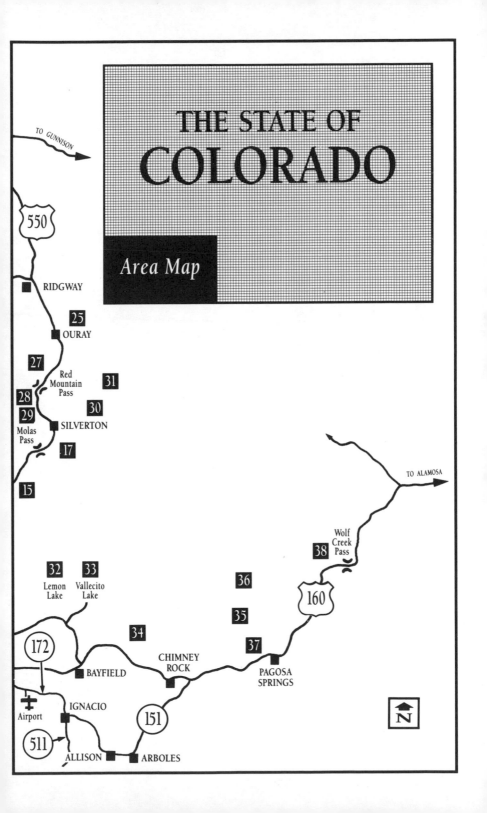

Snow and Terrain

The forests of southwestern Colorado have much to say to the cross-country skier. The trees tell of a huge range of altitude zones and a wide variety of snow conditions. To the skier who pays attention, the trees have information to convey about slope aspect and avalanche danger. Beyond terrain facts, the forests also communicate the beauty of nature; perhaps this, most of all, is what draws ski tourers to the backcountry again and again.

Pinyon pine and juniper are the characteristic trees of the lowest elevation zone traversed by any of these ski tours. Snow deep enough for skiing is intermittent throughout the winter at altitudes of 6500-7000 feet (2000-2150 meters), limited primarily to periods of a few days immediately following snowstorms. In the pinyon-juniper zone, the skier makes ephemeral tracks on the borderline between the mountains and the desert, an experience whose uniqueness is ensured by its rarity.

The handful of ski routes in this book which pass through pinyon-juniper areas are all easy. They present no avalanche danger because a deep snowpack does not form in this elevation zone.

In the next higher altitude zone, 7000-8500 feet (2150-2600 meters), ponderosa pine and gambel oak areas provide a wealth of skiing opportunities which are easily accessible. The snowslide danger is minimal on most routes in the pine-oak belt. The snow cover is adequate for skiing primarily in the deep winter months of mid-December to February. Pine-oak areas can also have good skiing following big snowstorms from late November through March.

Ponderosa pine forests are often fairly open, providing opportunities to wander off of roads and trails and find either wild solitude or interesting downhill pitches. Gambel oak, in contrast, forms impenetrable thickets of brush which skiers will be glad to avoid by following the routes of roads which cut through it. On northern slopes, Douglas fir grows in this elevation zone, indicating a cooler micro-climate with better snow conditions than southern slopes. Most ski routes in the pine-oak belt are suitable for beginners, though there are also hilly sections which can challenge more advanced skiers.

Forest roads provide skiers with easy-to-follow routes which frequently climb through more than one altitude zone. The national forests do not do any snowplowing, though portions of some forest roads are plowed by counties or private landowners with adjacent property.

Ascending above 8500 feet (2600 meters), the skier enters the extensive aspen forests which are characteristic of the San Juan Mountains. Good skiing here typically begins in December, though big snowstorms may bring skiing in as early as mid-November. The first part of April is about as late as you can count on skiing in the aspen.

Winter is a bright time of year in the aspen groves. The white forest floor reflects the sunshine which the leafless trees admit. In many aspen areas, the skiing is easy on gentle terrain. There is, however, no lack of steeper slopes for more advanced skiers. Forest roads, easy to follow in aspen woods, make good routes at moderate grades; open meadows between aspen groves become winter playgrounds.

Avalanche danger in the aspen belt is most significant where slidepaths, which may extend all the way down from above treeline, reach this zone. Slopes of thirty degrees or more, whether open or thinly forested, also represent danger when unstable snow conditions exist.

Above the aspen woodlands, coniferous forests cover higher slopes of the San Juans from 10,000-11,500 feet (3050-3500 meters). In the shade of Engelmann spruce and subalpine fir the snowpack is deep and long-lasting; here the skier will find many opportunities for memorable touring and turning. Backcountry tourers speak of the "tree powder" in this zone in hushed tones and with a faraway look in their eyes. The most consistently excellent ski conditions in the region are found in these spruce-fir forests.

I like the rather poetic term "boreal forest" (for Boreas, Greek god

Boreal Forest, Taylor Mesa.

of the north wind) as a name for this zone. Ski touring among the evergreens often takes me in spirit to Alaska or Canada, Scandinavia or northern Minnesota — places, like these Colorado forests, where snow and spruce trees share some great mystery in silence. Deep in the wilderness, firs decorated with snow glitter like Christmas trees in groves which extend for many miles.

Steep slopes in the boreal forest zone attract advanced skiers who can make narrow-radius turns between the trees. More moderate slopes and open meadows in this elevation zone offer novice and intermediate skiers enjoyable terrain. The summits of the mountain passes reached by highways in southwestern Colorado are in the spruce-fir belt, as are many of the slopes of Telluride, Purgatory, and Wolf Creek downhill ski areas. The backcountry skiing season in the coniferous forest may begin early in November, before the downhill ski areas open, and last well into April or early May after they have closed.

Numerous areas of high avalanche danger exist in the spruce-fir zone. Snowslides are quite capable of running through the trees as well as down the obvious slidepaths which cut wide swaths through the high-altitude forest. Trees with no branches on the uphill side of their trunks are indication that avalanches have run through the area in which they are growing.

3

Highest of all southwestern Colorado is the alpine tundra zone where the trees say much by their absence. In the San Juan Mountains this rugged environment typically lies above 11,500 feet (3500 meters) in elevation.

For the skier, the country above treeline holds many rewards. The ski season extends from October into June, giving the lie to the concept of skiing as a "winter" sport. There are many areas with moderate, wide-open slopes and incredible vistas. Being on the snow-covered tundra has always made me feel as I do when I stand at the edge of the sea; the scale and grandeur are truly oceanic.

The hazards of skiing above treeline, however, are as great as the rewards. Steep terrain is often unavoidable and the danger of snowslides is frequently high. Skiing the alpine tundra generally requires intermediate to advanced technique of those who would approach it safely. The ability to descend a steep slope under control may become a survival skill in rapidly changing weather or avalanche conditions. Overall physical fitness and acclimatization to the high altitude are also important.

Avalanche safety training is essential for skiers who plan to venture above treeline and into steep forested areas. Skiers without such training should tour in groups with experienced leadership.

Much alpine tundra skiing is best done in the spring. The mountain snowpack, warmed and softened by spring sunshine, refreezes and becomes stable during clear nights. Early in the morning, the snowslide danger is minimal. When mid-morning sun has just begun to soften the top of the snowpack, the skiing conditions on corn snow can be excellent. By afternoon, however, the avalanche danger may be very high.

Midwinter conditions on the alpine tundra are much different. Avalanche danger may be high at any time of the day or night, with wind, temperature, and snowfall as key factors to consider. On summits and ridges exposed to the wind, the snow gets packed hard as cement. Sun-crust frequently forms on south-facing slopes. On the other hand, the deep snow cover and frequency of fresh snow can make for first-rate skiing.

The San Juans have many jeep roads and pack trails which go above treeline, but these generally disappear beneath the deep snowpack in winter. Summer trails may also traverse areas which present extreme avalanche danger in winter, for example, steep slopes beneath ridges where cornices form. For these reasons, four-wheel-drive roads and trails shown on topographic maps do not necessarily make feasible ski routes.

Winter restores the wildness of primeval times to the high country, erasing much evidence of human intrusion. Areas which hikers can enjoy as a Sunday stroll in July become challenging wilderness adventures in December.

From the pinyon-juniper forest of the Ruins Road in Mesa Verde National Park to the alpine tundra of the 13,510-foot (4118-meter) summit of "Black Bear Peak," the ski tours in this book span an elevation range of over 6000 feet (1800 meters). These routes will lead you into the wonderland of nature in winter, and, more than once, give you glimpses of southwestern Colorado's past. Ghost towns, Anasazi ruins, and a white wilderness which in winter returns to its pre-human primitiveness await cross-country skiers who answer the call to adventure and set forth on the ski tours of southwestern Colorado.

○

Explanation of Trail Ratings

THE HEADINGS

If the skiing location being discussed is a ski touring center or area with groomed trails, this is mentioned first. For touring centers, elevation change, high point, and avalanche danger, headings are dropped and headings for trail fee, equipment rental charges, and telephone number are added.

DISTANCE

Unless otherwise specified, all distances are for the round trip. One-way distances (labelled as such) are given for the several tours which end at different places from where they start. Distances for these one-way tours do not include mileage back along the road to the starting point; this is given at the end of the tour description.

Where a range is given, for example "8-16 miles (12.4-25.6 kilometers)," it means there is more than one possible destination or turnaround point for the ski tour. The mileages for the shorter and longer options are listed.

Any tour can be shortened by simply going partway and turning back; most of the trips listed in this book will still be rewarding ski tours if done in this fashion. For this reason, I have included a number of tours with long mileages. Southwestern Colorado's many endurance athletes have the opportunity to go the distance, and casual recreational tourers will find plenty to reward them however many miles they go.

I have given distances in metric units in the headings, but not in the text, because putting all those numbers in parentheses interferes with readability. Here are some conversion factors for distances commonly mentioned in the text:

100 feet	=	30.5 meters
100 yards	=	91 meters
⅒th mile	=	⅙th kilometer
¼ mile	=	0.4 kilometers
½ mile	=	0.8 kilometers
¾ mile	=	1.2 kilometers
one mile	=	1.6 kilometers

STARTING ELEVATION

A tour which ascends from 11,000 feet to 13,000 feet is more difficult than a tour which makes the same 2000-foot climb from 7000 feet to 9000 feet. For this reason, and as a clue to snow conditions, the elevation above sea level at which a ski tour starts is often given.

ELEVATION CHANGE

Can routes which go up and down as much as the ones in this book be called "cross-country" skiing? The answer has to be yes if the country you are crossing is the San Juan Mountains. Then "up-and-down-country" skiing might indeed be the more exact description.

If not otherwise specified, the figure given for "elevation change" is the amount of elevation you will climb first and then come back down. This is the most common pattern among the ski tours in this book.

Some tours, however, end lower than they began. The Coalbank Pass Power Line Run even has the nerve to be all downhill. In these cases I specify the amounts of uphill and downhill either in the heading or in the text. With a situation like that of the Bear Creek tour, which goes up, down, back up, and back down, I just add up the totals for uphill and downhill and explain it all in the text.

As with the distance heading, elevation change may show a range, for example "500-1500 feet (152-457 meters)." If this is the case, the lesser elevation change goes with the shorter distance of a tour which goes just part of the way.

The amount of elevation change has a lot to do with the difficulty of a tour. A climb of over 500 feet in a mile feels steep on skis. The same vertical gain spread over five miles feels flat and easy. A climb of 2000 feet on skis is hard work no matter how you spread it out.

The amount of vertical drop when your return trip is a descent makes a big difference in the time it takes you to get home. On some trails, the trip down can be made in one-eighth the time of the climb. Trails like this, of course, are fairly steep routes suitable for intermediate to advanced skiers.

HIGH POINT

For high points which have some special significance, like peaks, ridges, or the end points of climbs of 1000 feet or more, the elevation is given in the heading. If the high point is just the end of a gradual rise with no special prominence, it is not mentioned in the heading; you can figure it out from the map or by adding the elevation change to the starting elevation. The high point heading may show a range, for example "11,240-11,920 feet (3426-3633 meters)," in which case the lower high point goes with the option for a shorter tour with less elevation gain.

RATING

Each route is rated for level of difficulty. Some routes are easy at first, then more difficult farther along. For these, a rating like "Novice-Intermediate" indicates that novice skiers can handle the first part of a route even though it requires intermediate ability to ski to the end. When the distance and elevation headings indicate more than one option for a tour, the shorter option with less elevation gain will generally correspond to the part of the tour rated less difficult. I use four basic categories for skill levels among cross-country skiers: beginner, novice, intermediate, and advanced.

The difficulty level of a trail is greatly affected by snow conditions. In rating each trail, I had in mind neither the best nor the worst of possible snow conditions but rather something in the middle. On hard, icy crust, routes rated "beginner" will topple most beginners and routes rated "intermediate" will demand advanced skill. In six inches of light powder, novices can descend grades usually requiring intermediate skill and intermediates can handle steep pitches usually reserved for advanced skiers.

"Beginner" as I use it means specifically someone who is putting cross-country skis on for the first time. Athletes from other sports who are just getting around to trying cross-country skiing may well be able to handle routes rated "novice" right away. An active athlete's sense of balance and coordination can make the transition to ski touring easy. Alpine skiers, in particular, will find that a certain amount of skill at getting down hills transfers from one type of skiing to another.

Non-athletes putting Nordic skis on for the first time usually struggle with their balance the first several times they ski and find the slightest downgrade horrifying. We were all there once. Times given for routes rated "beginner" presume a relatively slow pace.

"Novice" as I use it corresponds to the "easiest" or green-circle classification used at touring centers and on downhill ski slopes. Novice skiers have hopefully had a lesson or two, or at least some instruction from more experienced friends. The skier moves from beginner to novice when he or she begins to feel comfortable on the skis and can perform, not necessarily gracefully, a basic repertoire of techniques.

Novice skiers can kick-and-glide on the flat, sidestep or herring-bone up short steep spots, and stay in control on gentle downgrades by snowplowing or step-turning. They should know how to double-pole on slight downhills. Novices should be able to kick-turn, though I consider going up or down steep slopes with a series of traverses and kick-turns to be more in the intermediate category. And then there is that single most timeless and essential of ski techniques: the schuss, going straight down the hill. You can get a lot of mileage out of it on the slopes of novice routes because they are seldom so steep that you have to turn to stay in control.

Novice skiers who have been active in other sports may have the strength and endurance to attempt intermediate routes. If you are con-sidering testing your skill this way, read the trail description carefully. Intermediate routes with long, relatively steep downhills will not be much fun for novices who get in over their heads and just fall a lot.

"Intermediate" skiers are those to whom all the techniques above have become second nature. In addition, they are presumed to be capable of using kick-turns and traverses to handle steep slopes. Side-slipping down steep pitches is another intermediate technique. The half-snowplow, or "feather" turn, feathering one ski out and weighting it to turn, should be in the intermediate's repertoire. Skiers in this cate-gory are presumed to possess the endurance to go longer distances and make greater ascents than novice skiers.

The intermediate category corresponds to the "More Difficult" or blue square rating used by touring centers and downhill ski areas. As used in this book, it applies to routes with natural obstacles like logs in the trail, stream crossings, and bumpy terrain which require some agility to deal with on skis.

Strong intermediate skiers can make it along many of the advanced routes in this book, especially if snow conditions ·are favorable. The intermediate skier doing this will probably have to traverse down steep slopes that the advanced skier can descend with a series of turns down the fall line. This makes a descent take significantly longer for the inter-

Lewis McCool descending La Plata Canyon Road using the half-snowplow or "feather" turn, an intermediate technique.

mediate. On the other hand, skiing uphill is a plodding activity which an intermediate with a good level of endurance can do just as fast as an advanced skier.

As intermediate skiers gain more experience, they begin to learn how to handle steeper slopes with christies and rudimentary parallel turns. Routes rated "intermediate" in this book sometimes have down-hill pitches where these turns will get you by, but telemarks will make it more graceful. No intermediate route absolutely requires telemarking, but many provide a chance for skiers beginning to telemark to practice.

"Advanced" skiers are expected to be able to descend slopes approaching or exceeding twenty degrees with linked narrow-radius turns. For most, this will mean telemarking, though I have seen some advanced skiers do remarkably well with parallel turns on Nordic skis. There is a presumption that by the time a skier has reached this level of technique, he or she will be equipped for extensive backcountry travel and avalanche safety. A high level of physical fitness and complete acclimatization to high altitude are also assumed. Trails rated "advanced" in this book require route-finding ability and experience of the skier more often than lower-rated routes.

This category corresponds to the "Most Difficult" or black diamond rating used at touring centers and downhill ski areas. Generally speaking, however, the black diamond trails at a touring center are no comparison to the level of difficulty of advanced ski routes in the back-country. Skiers capable of doing linked telemark turns down black diamond runs at the downhill ski areas, however, almost certainly have adequate technique for steep backcountry skiing. Slopes traveled by Nordic skiers in the backcountry seldom exceed the steepness of inter-mediate runs at downhill ski areas. Backcountry slopes, however, do present a more challenging variety of snow and terrain conditions.

TIME ALLOWED

When a range is given, for example "4-8 hours," the shorter time goes with the option for a tour of less distance and less elevation change which may also have an easier skill rating. All times are only estimates which are based on a middle ground with respect to snow conditions. If you find your group breaking trail in two feet of new snow, you may take three times as long as the "time allowed" heading estimates. If you are out with a group of athletes who charge up the hill and descend with excellent downhill control, you can cut some of these times in half.

In clocking ski tours on some of the routes, I found that two miles per hour seemed to keep coming up as an average, even for routes with quite a bit of vertical change. Slow, hard climbs were compensated for by the rapidity of the descent. I have tried to be generous in

Kristi Nichols telemarking in U.S. Basin, an advanced technique.

estimating these time allowances, but being unable to foresee snow conditions and not knowing your pace as a skier really make my best efforts pure guesswork.

AVALANCHE DANGER

See the following chapter on avalanche safety, which includes information on the basis for the avalanche danger ratings given for each tour.

MAPS

Where a 7.5' (read "seven and one-half minute") quadrangle topographic map shows the ski route, it is the preferred map due to its level of detail. The quadrangles mentioned are generally the base maps used in preparing the route maps in this guide; you may still want the whole quad for the identification of distant landforms, the additional information supplied by color, or better detail on the maps which have been reduced to fit this book. I highly recommend that you use the original topo map quad on any route whose text in this book mentions route-finding challenges.

Some forest roads show only on the non-topographic Forest Service Map; if this is the case, that map is mentioned. Where a topographic county map is mentioned, it is because the entire ski route shows on its larger scale while two or more 7.5' maps are required.

The San Juan National Forest 1985 Travel Map is a good companion to this book. It gives an overview of the whole area spanned by this guide with the exception of Ouray (shown on the Uncompahgre National Forest Map). This map, available at all San Juan National Forest offices, is an excellent aid to finding the trailheads to the tours in this book since it shows highways, county roads, and Forest Service roads. The regular San Juan National Forest Map is on a slightly larger scale than the 1985 Travel Map and uses color to show land ownership more clearly, but it is not as up-to-date on forest roads.

TRAIL MAP LEGEND

Main ski route ■ ■ ■ ■ ■ ■ ■ ■ ■ ■ ■

Side trip or option ■ ■ ■ ● ● ● ● ● ● ● ●

Avalanche hazard .... ●

Some Comments on Equipment

Any type of cross-country ski, even racing or skating skis, will get you around on the beginner and novice routes. Racing and skating skis, which are designed for skiing in prepared tracks, will of course do their best at the touring centers.

For intermediate and advanced routes, metal-edged backcountry skis will give you the most versatility for dealing with varied slopes and snow conditions. Skis without edges will suffice on the intermediate routes under most snow conditions; the edges, however, are a great help in icy or crusty conditions, even on forest roads.

A somewhat stiff and high-ankled boot is the most versatile for backcountry routes. A compromise between comfort during flat touring and downhill control must inevitably be made.

Climbing skins are useful on many routes (above the novice level) with long, fairly steep to very steep upgrades. In winter conditions — cold fresh snow — waxes work well even for steep climbs. In spring snow (settled and relatively warm), skins are far more convenient than klisters.

Appropriate clothing is important to your comfort on the trail. In southwestern Colorado, you can be skiing in a T-shirt at the start of a tour and need a heavy parka an hour later when it clouds over and starts snowing. A snowproof outer layer is always essential, but the ability to take layers off to avoid getting sweaty and later chilled is equally important.

Windbreakers worn over down vests and ski sweaters make good layers. An outer layer of gaiters and knickers on your legs is highly recommended. Long underwear is not recommended for the sunny southwest; it is a hot layer which is hard to shed if you overheat. A hat which packs easily, like a knit cap, and gloves are always important. Sunscreen and sunglasses are highly recommended.

Carry a warm pair of mittens on longer tours. An insulating survival blanket ("space" blanket) is also useful; it can be used as a seat in the snow. Ski goggles are occassionally helpful in blizzard conditions. A ski tip, tools, screws, and glue for binding repairs should be carried by someone in the group on long backcountry excursions.

On routes which pass through avalanche terrain, carry a collapsible shovel. It can be used to dig a snowpit and get out of the wind for comfort as well as for avalanche safety. Ski poles which convert into avalanche probes are a sensible precaution, as are radio beacons. A full avalanche safety kit will include flagging to mark location clues in the event of an avalanche burial, a backpacking stove to warm liquids for an avalanche hypothermia victim, a pup tent or sleeping bag for the same purpose, and avalanche cords. Other items which professional rescue personnel carry include means of making a sled to transport a victim, ropes, and first aid kit.

O

Avalanche Safety

The information below should be read by all skiers planning to ski routes listed in this book which have avalanche danger ratings of "moderate" or "high."

Colorado Avalanche Information Center (CAIC)
303 236-9435 (Denver)

Slopes which have the potential for avalanche danger exist along many of the ski routes of southwestern Colorado. Neither the author nor the publisher assumes any liability for the safety of any skier using any of the routes described in this book.

This book reports on routes that have been skied and areas which have the potential to be skied. The decision on when and where to ski is always 100 percent the personal responsibility of the skier. A reasonable effort has been made to provide skiers with information about hazards as an aid to making decisions as to when and where to ski safely. There may, however, be hazards along these ski routes in addition to those mentioned.

Ski tours in this book which have an avalanche danger rating of "low" pass through terrain where snowslides seldom, if ever, occur. The simplest method of avoiding avalanche danger is to ski only these routes.

To ski safely on routes which have an avalanche danger rating of "moderate," skiers should be able to recognize avalanche terrain and should be aware of the level of avalanche danger at the time they are skiing. To ski safely on routes which have an avalanche danger rating of "high," skiers should be very familiar with avalanche terrain recognition and be equipped for avalanche rescue. In addition they should be capable of performing snowpit analysis, observing snow mechanics, and applying both short-term and long-term weather information to a determination of the level of snowslide danger on the specific slopes thay plan to ski. Skiers without this level of avalanche safety expertise and equipment should not ski routes rated "high" in avalanche danger unless they are in a group with experienced leadership.

The Colorado Avalanche Information Center (CAIC), in coopera- tion with the U.S. Forest Service, maintains an avalanche information hotline at the number listed above. Updated daily from November through April with reports from avalanche observers across the state, it is an authoritative source of information on the current level of avalanche danger in Colorado mountain areas.

Interpreting the taped message and applying it to a specific area where you may ski requires knowledge of the terrain and of avalanche phenomena. Slab avalanches pose the greatest potential threat to skiers. Hard slab, soft slab, and wet slab avalanches all occur in the San Juan Mountains. Hard slab avalanches most frequently result from the accumulation of windblown snow. Soft slab avalanches occur when new snow adheres poorly to the older snow beneath it in the snow- pack. Wet slab avalanches in the San Juans occur in the spring, primar- ily after late morning, as sunlight and warm temperatures loosen up the snowpack and lubricate surfaces within or beneath it with melt- water. Another type of avalanche, the point release, poses less of a threat to skiers because it seldom moves enough snow to bury a person. Snow stability conditions are highly variable, depending on slope aspect, elevation, and current weather conditions.

The CAIC telephone report will rate the overall avalanche danger as "extreme," "high," "moderate," or "low." Tours in this book with an avalanche danger rating of "high" should not be skied when the CAIC rates the avalanche danger level as "extreme," "high," or "moderate." Informed judgement should be exercised in deciding whether or not to ski these areas at any time. Even when the CAIC reports the ava- lanche danger level as "low," avalanches may occur in areas which this book rates as having high potential for avalanche danger.

Slab avalanche, west side of Ophir Pass.

Any route in this book which crosses, climbs, or descends open slopes approaching or exceeding 30 degrees is given an avalanche danger rating of "high." These slopes will feel steep to a cross-country skier. Any tour which traverses the steep track (or "acceleration zone") of an obvious slidepath, where a skier could trigger a slide, is rated "high" in potential avalanche danger.

Tours in this book with an avalanche danger rating of "moderate" should not be skied when the CAIC reports the avalanche danger as "extreme" or "high," and informed judgement should be exercised in deciding whether to ski these areas in times when the CAIC rates the avalanche danger level as "moderate." Generally speaking, tours in this book with an avalanche danger rating of "moderate" should be safe to ski when the CAIC rates avalanche danger as "low," but the factors of weather, elevation, and slope aspect must be evaluated for each specific time and location.

Any tour in this book which crosses a recognizable slidepath, even in relatively flat terrain in its runout zone, is given an avalanche danger rating of at least "moderate." Routes which put the skier near to open slopes approaching or exceeding 30 degrees, but not actually on them, are also rated at least "moderate" in avalanche danger potential.

The CAIC telephone avalanche report may specify the level of danger for regions within the state. The tours in this book are all in the southern mountain region of Colorado. The telephone report may also be specific about terrain, for example, "avalanche danger is high for south-facing slopes of thirty-five degrees or more above treeline." Use this information in conjunction with the route description and the map to determine whether your planned tour includes areas of particularly high danger. Frequently the avalanche danger is higher above treeline than below treeline.

TO SKI OR NOT TO SKI

Four basic factors enter into the decision as to whether it is safe or unsafe at any given time to ski in avalanche terrain. The following summary details observations which give you some clues about the level of avalanche danger. For more comprehensive information, avalanche safety courses which include field experience are recommended.

1
Weather

Snow which falls at the rate of an inch an hour or more in the area where you might ski creates high avalanche danger when the accumulation of new snow exceeds six inches. The danger persists for 24 to 48 hours after the storm stops, and possibly longer if there are unstable layers deep in the snowpack. The CAIC telephone report includes a mountain weather forecast which is tailored specifically to high-elevation areas.

High winds increase avalanche danger, especially on lee slopes where windblown snow accumulates. The wind can be presumed to be dangerously high if it is strong enough to obviously move snow. Wind strong enough to sway treetops or send snow banners streaming from peaks and ridges also increases avalanche danger.

Rapid temperature changes during or just after a snowstorm can increase the avalanche danger. A rise in temperature during a snowstorm deposits heavy wet snow on top of lighter cold snow, destabilizing the snowpack. Rapid warming, which can occur when new snow is heated by exposure to sunlight in late winter and early spring, can also create instability. On the other hand, a stable, relatively warm temperature during and after a storm tends to favor the settling and stabilization of snow, making the danger of avalanches low.

Extreme cold which persists during and after new snowfall or following a period of high winds is a danger sign. When the temperature stays well below freezing, this tends to prevent new or windblown snow from settling and stabilizing.

Spring weather brings a cycle of wet avalanches to the San Juan Mountains. The occurence of these wet slab avalanches relates directly to increasing warmth, with exposure to sunlight as a major factor. Early in spring, the snow on south- and east-facing slopes will soften up in the sun earlier in the morning than the snow on slopes with other aspects.

2
Snow Mechanics

Settling of snow with a "whooshing" noise as you ski across it indicates the collapse of a weak layer within the snowpack. If the snow above the collapsing layer is dense enough to form a slab and there is a slippery surface in the snowpack beneath the slab, the avalanche danger is high.

Cracking of the snow as you ski across it is a danger sign, as are natural fracture lines in the snowpack on slopes around you. When cracks or fractures in the snow occur on steep slopes, they place a stress on the snowpack which can initiate an avalanche.

3

Snowpit Analysis

The only way to observe layers buried in the snowpack is to dig a hole in the snow. Carrying a collapsible shovel is highly recommended for travel in avalanche terrain both for its use in digging a snowpit and for possible rescue work.

Dig a pit and shear snow off of one side to make a vertical wall. Several quick tests then give you a wealth of information about the snowpack. Running a credit card edgewise down through the snowpack detects hard layers which might act as bedding planes for slabs above to slide along. Carving out a pillar of snow from the wall and using the shovel to push sideways on each layer to see if it slides off the layer below is the "shovel shear" test.

Poking your fist, fingers, a pencil, or a knife in each layer tells you how dense the snow is. A fist will penetrate "depth hoar," cohesionless snow which forms weak, collapsing layers within the snowpack. A fist will also penetrate "champagne powder," low-density fresh snow. Low-density snow which accumulates rapidly and forms a deep layer can trigger slab avalanches. Layers of denser snow, requiring four fingers or even one finger to penetrate them, need not be as deep to trigger snowslides due to their greater weight. The densest snow — capable of forming hard slab avalanches if weak or sliding layers exist beneath it — can only be penetrated by a pencil or a knife.

In the snowpit, you determine what the layers are in the snowpack and how well they are bonded together. Snow of density sufficient to form a slab which is on the top of a slippery or collapsing layer indicates a high probability of slab avalanches. The snowpack may vary

Shovel shear test being performed by Betsy Armstrong at the 1987 Silverton Avalanche School.

substantially on slopes of different aspects and elevations; ideally, your snowpit should be dug on a slope like the one which you plan to ski. Avoid exposing yourself to danger when digging the snowpit, however.

If every layer in the snowpack is bonded to every other layer, including the ground below, as if they were glued together, the snowpack in that particular area is "bombproof." Not even explosives trigger snowslides on steep slopes under such conditions. This is the exception rather than the rule in the San Juans, but at such times it is safe to ski in avalanche terrain.

4
Terrain Recognition

Slopes of 30 to 45 degrees present the greatest potential for avalanche danger. Slopes of 20 to 30 degrees are steep enough to produce snowslides under very high hazard conditions. A device called an inclinometer (slope meter) can be used to measure slope angles precisely; they are hard to judge accurately by eye. A 30-degree slope is very steep for Nordic skiing; only advanced telemarkers can ski down the fall line on such a grade. Even 20-degree slopes are steep for cross-country skis.

Slope aspect has an effect on avalanche potential. In the San Juan Mountains, sun-crust forms frequently on open south-facing slopes. The crust can serve as a sliding surface for a slab above. The most common prevailing wind in the San Juans is from a westerly direction; this will tend to wind-load eastern, northeastern, and southeastern slopes. Cornices, whose falling can trigger slab avalanches, tend to hang over the east-facing side of ridges because of wind-loading from the west. The skier, however, must always be alert for potential hazards in any direction, particularly from above.

The obvious slidepaths seen at many locations can be divided into three zones. At the top is the starting zone, down the slope is the track or acceleration zone, and at the bottom is the runout zone. The runout zone may be flat or a gentle slope; the starting zone and track are generally steep slopes. Skiers are most likely to trigger a slide by skiing in the starting zone or the track.

The presence of avalanche debris on a slidepath may indicate that everything which is going to slide has come down, in which case the slidepath is safe. On the other hand, the skier must evaluate the possibility that more unstable snow remains above, especially if the slidepath has multiple starting zones.

One of the most important practical indications of avalanche danger in any kind of avalanche terrain is the presence of debris from recent slides. If some slopes of a given angle and aspect have avalanched but other slopes with similar angle and aspect have not, the similar slopes where avalanches have not yet occurred should be avoided. The odds are that they represent potential avalanches waiting only for additional weight, like a skier, to trigger them.

Steep-walled stream gullies are dangerous places for skiers. Snow avalanching off the sides, even if the walls are only ten feet high, will pile up deep in the gully bottom since it has no place to spread out.

FOR FURTHER READING

LaChappele, E.R. **The ABC of Avalanche Safety.** *The Mountaineers, Seattle, 1985.*

A compact paperback, highly recommended. Read it through twice and carry it in your pack.

Armstrong, Betsy and Williams, Knox. **The Avalanche Book.** *Fulcrum Incorporated, Golden, Colorado, 1986.*

Knox Williams is the present director of the Colorado Avalanche Information Center and Betsy Armstrong is the former associate director.

Daffern, Tony. **Avalanche Safety for Skiers and Climbers.** *Alpenbooks, Seattle, 1983.*

Fraser, Colin. **Avalanches and Snow Safety.** *Charles Scribner's Sons, New York, 1978.*

U.S. Dept. of Agriculture Handbook No. 489, **Avalanche Handbook.** *Washington, D.C., 1978.*

> Very technical but authoritative; "handbook" is a misnomer for such a weighty volume. Available through U.S. Government Printing Office.

Avalanches occur along the highways which cross mountain passes in southwestern Colorado. The Colorado State Highway Patrol maintains a recorded telephone message which tells you whether slides have closed the road at Coalbank, Molas, Red Mountain, Lizard Head, or Wolf Creek passes. It will also tell you if travel on the passes is restricted to vehicles with adequate snow tires or chains due to snow conditions. Four-wheel-drive vehicles with mud-and-snow tires having at least one-eighth inch of tread depth are in compliance with the Colorado chain law.

Colorado State Highway Patrol road conditions report

303 247-3355 (Durango)

303 565-4511 (Cortez)

O

Areas in and Near Durango

Durango would only be a small town anywhere else, but in lightly populated southwestern Colorado, it is the biggest city. A goodly number of cross-country skiers, from casual recreational types to diehard backcountry telemarkers, call it home. The city has a number of ski shops which offer rental and repair services for both cross-country and downhill equipment. Pine Needle Mountaineering in the Main Mall near 8th Street and Main Avenue carries the largest selection of backcountry skiing gear.

A skier need not go far from Main Avenue to find good back-country touring. The areas close to the city are in the pinyon-juniper and ponderosa pine-oak brush altitude zones, which means that snow cover is most likely to be good from mid-December through February or just after big storms from late November through March. Avalanche danger in all these areas is low to nonexistant. The touring is generally easy, though there are some grades which require intermediate skiing ability, and short slopes steep enough for telemarking can be found in a few spots.

O

Hillcrest Golf Course

Maintained track
Distance: 1.6 miles (2.5 kilometers)
Starting elevation: 6800 feet (2060 meters)
Elevation change: Slight
Rating: Beginner - Novice
Time allowed: 1 hour
Avalanche danger: None
Maps: Not necessary

This maintained track, groomed whenever the snow is deep enough for skiing, is on the northern side of the Fort Lewis College campus on a mesa overlooking Durango. Use of the track is free and open to the public.

Since it is located in the sagebrush and pinyon-juniper zone, Hillcrest has a fairly short snow season. The deep winter months, late December through February, are most likely to provide good ski conditions. Days immediately after big snowstorms from November into March may also be good. Winter droughts, periods of two weeks or more without snow, are typical of Durango winters and sometimes render Hillcrest snowless in January.

Entrance to the course for skiing is restricted to the southwestern corner of the golf course, near a red shed with a sign on it. Park in the Fort Lewis College stadium lot a few hundred feet away. Dogs are not allowed on the course and skiers must stay in the groomed tracks. Do not ski the course when it is officially closed. Adherence to these few rules is a small price to pay for free access to groomed tracks.

The track consists of a one-mile loop around the perimeter of the golf course with a connecting trail through the center. Towards the far end (north) of the longer loop, there is a small hill. Beginning skiers should be able to handle this grade, both up and down, before heading for even the easiest routes at Molas Pass.

Hillcrest is a good place for first-time skiers (beginners) and those with little cross-country skiing experience (novices). The track is also used, however, by racers staying in shape; Nordic skiing etiquette asks that a slower skier always yield the track to a faster skier.

For more information call Durango Parks and Recreation at 303 247-5622 or Hillcrest Maintenance at 303 259-0424.

O

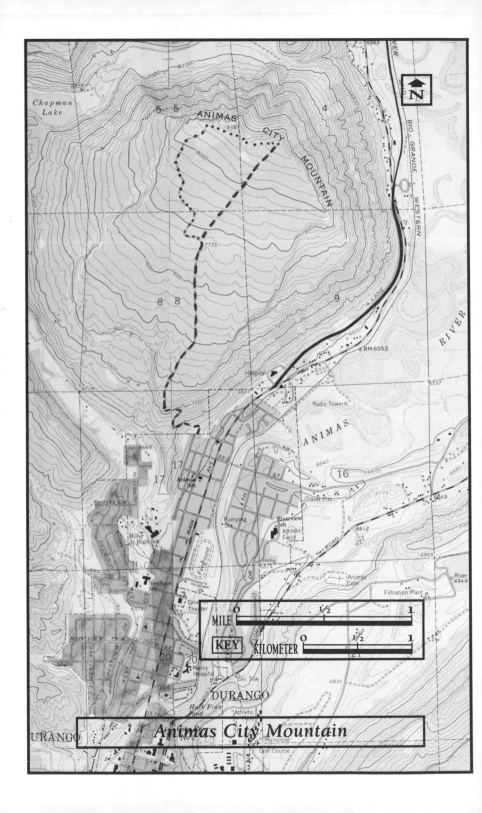

Animas City Mountain

Animas City Mountain

Distance: 5 miles (8 kilometers)
Starting elevation: 6680 feet (2036 meters)
Elevation change: 1480 feet (451 meters)
High point: 8160 feet (2487 meters)
Rating: Intermediate
Time allowed: 4 hours
Avalanche danger: Low
Maps: 7.5' Durango East
La Plata County (topographic) Sheet 2

The land beneath the ponderosa pines of Animas City Mountain is designated for wildlife habitat protection by the Bureau of Land Management. This is critical winter range for deer and elk, a scarce commodity in a time when human activities have disrupted age-old migration routes, feeding areas, and calving grounds.

To visit this winter home of the big game, take 32nd Street west from Main Avenue to its end at West 4th Avenue. Park near here and carry your skis north a couple of blocks on West 4th, where the paved street ends and a former jeep road continues on. The jeep road makes a switchback and starts up the mountainside just beyond a power substation.

This south-facing section of road seldom retains good snow cover. Skiing may be good in the forest above even though you have to hike the first half-mile of steep, rocky road carrying your skis. This short section would be a rough expert run even if it had enough snow to ski on, which is infrequent. Plan on walking both up and down it.

At the top of this first climb, which is steeper than anything that lies ahead, the route turns to the right. The ridge leading southwest (on your left as you make the turn) dead-ends in a quarter mile at a water tank.

The route followed by the former jeep road continues uphill for about 2 miles to a point on the northern rim of the mountain which overlooks the Falls Creek Valley. The actual summit of the mountain

Dave and Fran Hart admiring the view from the summit.

is east of this point. The uphill grade is not generally steep but it is sustained.

The summit of the mountain can be reached more directly by bearing right (northeast) from the jeep road after about a mile of ascent through the ponderosa pine forest. Picking a route between the pines and growths of oak brush is not difficult. Some say that this is the only real "cross-coutry" skiing, crossing the country without benefit of road or set tracks. It certainly puts the skier closer to the backcountry — too close, sometimes, to obstacles like tangles of brush and fallen logs.

From the summit, on the northeastern corner of the mountain, the view over the Animas Valley to the West Needle Mountains is dramatic. The ski run back down through the pines can be exciting as well. In snow which is fresh and soft your tracks speed your descent. On top of settled snow, you might find yourself slaloming the pines like a participant in some kind of wilderness Olympics.

○

3

Bodo State Wildlife Area

Distance: 10 miles (16 kilometers)
Starting elevation: 7200 feet (2195 meters)
Elevation change: 525 feet (160 meters)
High point: 7725 feet (2355 meters)
Rating: Novice - Intermediate
Time allowed: 6 hours
Avalanche danger: Low
Maps: 7.5' Basin Mountain
       7.5' Durango West

During or just after snowstorms, when the danger of avalanches is too high to ski in areas prone to snowslides, this tour gives the skier the opportunity to explore several miles of pine and juniper back-country. Snow cover is adequate for skiing primarily in deep winter, late December through February, or immediately after storms which deposit a foot or more of snow at 7000 feet.

The trailhead is on the Wildcat Canyon Road, which leads south from U.S. 160 two miles west of Durango. On the left side of the road 3.6 miles south from the 160 intersection, a little less than a mile beyond the Rafter J/Open A road on the right, there is a parking area big enough for two or three cars. This parking area is not plowed; roadside parking is possible as an alternative but always stay well off the road when snowplows are at work.

After passing through the fence and crossing a brook, continue in the same direction, uphill into fairly open ponderosa pine forest. Within one-quarter of a mile you reach the top of an east-west ridge. The remnant of an old road is here to guide you; bear left and follow it. If you miss it or lose it, simply stay on top of the ridge heading east.

There is ample evidence of human activity in this wildlife area. Power lines flank the ski route; south of and below the ridgetop, County Road 211 roughly parallels the ridge. The site for burial of Durango's uranium mill tailings is a few miles away (not close to this ski route) on the southern slopes of Smelter Mountain. Ridges Basin,

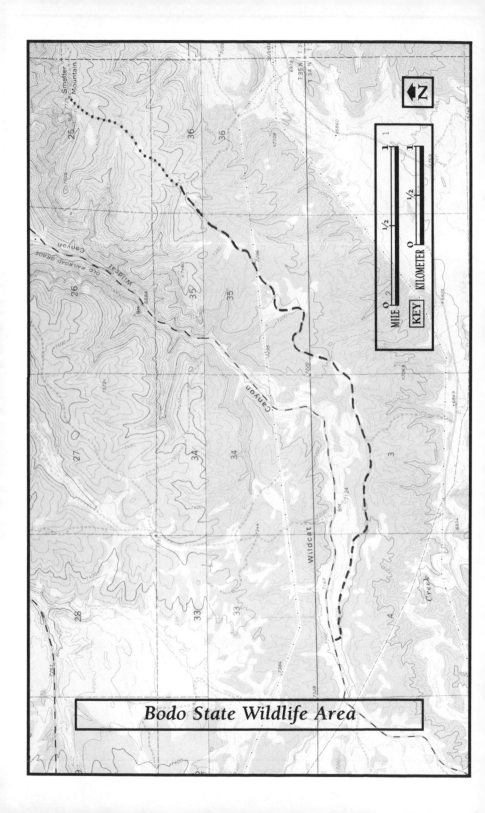

Bodo State Wildlife Area

*Gambel oak
in snow.*

south of the ridge you are skiing on, will be filled by the Animas-La Plata Reservoir if it is built. The Nature Conservancy had acquired this land, which was formerly part of the Bodo Ranch, in order to preserve it as wildlife habitat. As you ski here, you might think about the political expendability of wildlife conservation land in the face of the pressures of our technological society.

Continuing east along the ridgetop, you join a more distinct road-way within half a mile. At two forks in the road, stay left. Also stay left where a power line meets the road.

In spite of the intrusions of technology, elk still winter in this area. You should see their tracks and possibly those of pine marten, weasel, or cottontail rabbit as well. Perhaps there will be an Abert's squirrel in the pines, easily identified by its tufted ears.

The road leads you on gentle grades towards the western end of Smelter Mountain. As you come on to its south-facing slopes, you have the unusual experience of crossing from ponderosa pine-gambel oak to pinyon-juniper forest while gaining elevation. The southern exposure is what makes this possible here; it also keeps the ski season short at this location.

The road intersects County Road 212 at a red gate. Turning left here will take you to the top of Smelter Mountain in a bit under a mile. On top you are five miles from where you started. County Road 212 is used by motor vehicles in the winter for access to the radio towers on the mountaintop; it therefore may not be skiable except immediately after a storm. When it can be skied, it is a moderate climb to the summit which makes for a nice downhill grade on the return. Even if you have to take your skis off and walk, the trip to the summit is worthwhile for the striking view over Durango.

The time and distance given in the heading presume a return trip along the same route. Your own ski tracks blaze the trail home. Watch to see if elk have crossed them since you made them.

O

4

Perins Peak State Wildlife Area Routes

Starting elevation: 6960 feet (2121 meters)
Rating: Beginner - Intermediate
Avalanche danger: Low
Map: 7.5' Durango West

Between Barnroof Point on the west and Perins Peak on the east, the valley of the Dry Fork provides pleasant touring in ponderosa pine country. To reach it, take U.S. Highway 160 west 3.4 miles from Durango and turn right on Lightner Creek Road (County Road 207). One mile up Lightner Creek Road, the unplowed Dry Fork Road (County Road 208) goes straight ahead where plowed and paved Lightner Creek Road bears left. A parking area is plowed out here, though it is one of the last spots the plows get to after a storm. Roadside parking is also possible.

Ski north across the open meadow to start, or up the road if you wish. The road provides the easiest way to cross the gully of the Dry Fork a quarter mile in. Oak brush eventually prevents you from wandering too far from the road in any case. The grade is gently uphill for two miles with a couple of sections which are slightly steeper. This part of the road and the open fields adjacent to it are suitable for first-time cross-country skiers. At the two-mile point there is a fork in the road. The route to the left will lead you north of Barnroof Point; taking the right fork will start you on the Dry Fork to Durango route. These longer routes are suitable for intermediate skiers or for novices who do not mind walking short steep sections.

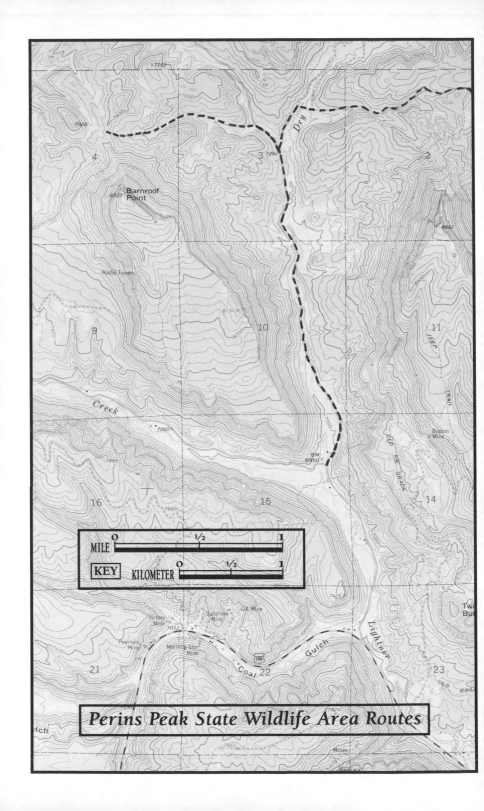

Perins Peak State Wildlife Area Routes

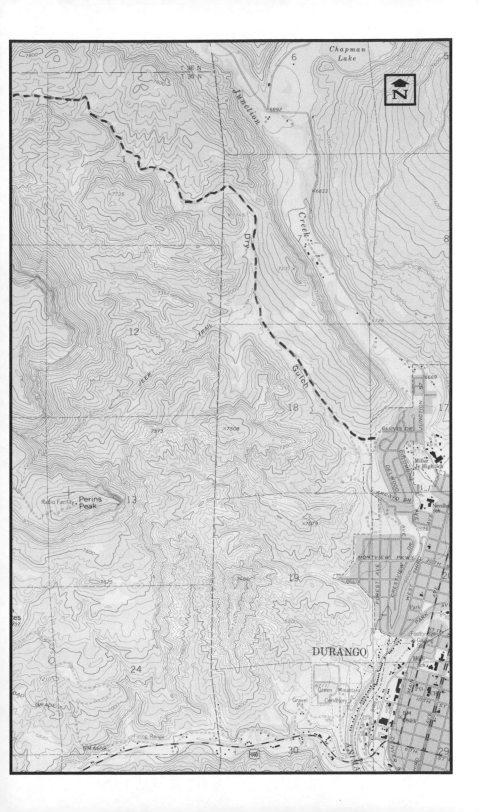

A

N O R T H   O F   B A R N R O O F   P O I N T

Distance: 6 miles (9.6 kilometers) round trip
    from Lightner Creek Road trailhead
Elevation change: 820 feet (250 meters)
High point: 7780 feet (2371 meters)
Time allowed: 3 hours

Heading left from the fork in the road, the route continues gently uphill for a quarter of a mile to an open field. Take a left again here and cross the fence to stay on public land. (The road straight ahead comes to a gate in a hundred yards; to continue beyond the gate would be trespassing on private land.) This left turn puts you on a trail which heads west and climbs gently up a little valley.

Continue up the valley for about a mile, uphill at a moderate grade all the way. You pass through stands of big, healthy-looking gambel oak which has attained the stature of small trees. At the head of the valley, a short, steep climb (quite challenging on skis) brings you to the top of a little ridge coming off the northern face of Barnroof Point. The view of the cliff on Barnroof is impressive, as is the view of the La Platas to the west.

The ridgetop is your turnaround point. The first few yards down are an expert run; a steep, narrow lane through thick oak brush. Most skiers will probably want to sidestep or walk down the first fifty feet. The lower portion of the steep pitch is a short intermediate run which will start your return trip with a bang. Novice skiers can walk down a little farther and still get some fun out of this bit of downhill. The gentle downhill grade for the rest of the way back will speed your return.

*First-time skier
Brenda Bailey
on the
Dry Fork Road.*

B

D R Y   F O R K   T O   D U R A N G O

Distance: 7 miles (11.2 kilometers)
High point: 7720 feet (2353 kilometers)
Elevation change: up 760 feet (232 meters),
    down 1000 feet (305 meters)
Time allowed: 4 hours

This route, if followed all the way to the end, leaves you on Clovis
Street in Durango, seven miles from the trailhead on Lightner Creek
Road. The Clovis Street end of the trail is reached by car by taking

25th Street west from Main Avenue in Durango. Take the second left after Miller Junior High School; this is Clovis Street. Follow Clovis Street for half a mile to its end on top of a hill where Borrego Drive joins it from the left. Straight ahead is the entrance to Rock Ridge Homesites which is the end of the ski route. Park a second car here or make arrangements to be picked up.

Heading right from the fork two miles up the road in the Perins Peak State Wildlife Area, the route drops slightly and continues one-quarter mile to a large open field on the right. Just before coming to a fence, take a right across this field. The route is hard to follow for the next quarter mile. It follows a summer trail which enters the woods at the northern end of the open field. Head east, following as best you can the opening in the brush and woods created by the summer trail, which is the remnant of a jeep road. Unfortunately, similar-looking openings in the woods can lead you astray. They inevitably peter out in oak brush; the correct route will continue uphill at a moderate grade for a mile to the high point of the route. The rocky face on the northern spur of Perins Peak is to your right.

This is the logical point at which to turn around if you want to return to your starting point instead of taking the one-way trip to Clovis Street. Turning back from the high point gives you a 6.8-mile tour (round trip) with 760 feet of elevation change.

Continuing east to Durango from the high point, it is 1000 feet downhill to Clovis Street. The trail is clear for a couple of miles. It drops fairly steeply for a couple of hundred yards and then more steeply around a couple of quite tricky curves. These require intermediate skiing ability, possible even advanced ability under fast snow conditions. This fairly short section is the only difficult part of the whole route.

After the steep drop, the route continues gently downhill and southeast, reaching open fields where the road ceases to guide you. At this point you are descending Dry Gulch. As the grade flattens out, you want to bear to the right and cross the field. You pick up a road which leads you across a cattle guard at the wildlife area boundary. The last mile to Clovis Street is on private land on a distinct roadway serving the Rock Ridge Homesites. Development of this area could restrict public access in the future.

O

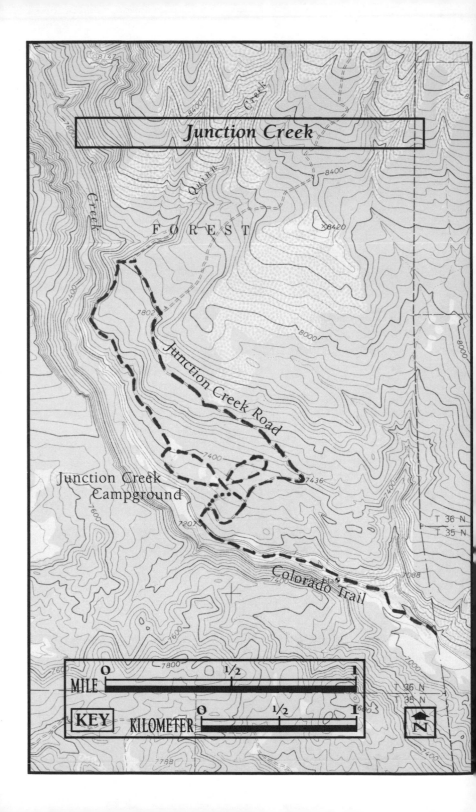

5

Junction Creek

Distance: 4-7 miles (6.4-11.2 kilometers)
Starting elevation: 7000 feet (2134 meters)
Elevation change: 280-800 feet (85-244 meters)
Rating: Novice - Intermediate
Time allowed: 3-5 hours
Avalanche danger: Low
Map: 7.5' Durango West

From 25th Street and Main Avenue in Durango, head west on 25th Street (which becomes Junction Street and then the Junction Creek Road). It is a 3.5-mile drive to the San Juan National Forest boundary at a cattle guard. Stay left at 2.9 miles where the road to Falls Creek Ranch branches off to the right. Snow plowing stops at the forest boundary. Do not park in the area where snowplows turn around; you will have to find space along the roadside which is out of their way.

The Junction Creek Road is popular with snowmobilers, but along the ski route you will be out of sight of them most of the time, if not out of earshot. Just after the forest boundary cattle guard, the ski trail heads left toward the creek. The first mile of trail is blazed with small square signs marked "X-C." This is the Durango end of the recently completed Colorado Trail.

For the first mile you stay to the right of the creek, below the road. This is pleasant skiing in a riparian environment of cottonwood trees. The canyon of Junction Creek becomes impressively steep-walled as you follow it upstream.

Just before the one-mile point, the trail forks. The branch uphill to the right returns you to the road; this is the main ski route. It is possible to continue along the branch to the left, though this crosses a section which is rough for skiing. This left branch will lead you to an open field west of the first hairpin turn in the Junction Creek Road.

After climbing up to the road on the right branch, you can follow the road half a mile, around the hairpin turn, to the main entrance of the Junction Creek Campground which will be on your left. The four

45

campground loops all provide easy skiing in the ponderosa pine forest. From the end of the "A" loop there is a nice hundred-yard downhill run back to the hairpin which you can use on your return trip; it may require intermediate skill in fast snow conditions.

The campground tour represents the turnaround point for beginner skiers and the shorter distance, time, and elevation gain given in the heading. Intermediate skiers may continue on a longer, rougher route which requires a good two-foot snow cover to be worth attempting. Such snow cover is not typical for this area, but may exist during periods of unusually heavy snowfall.

Opposite campground site C5, the remnant of an old road heads uphill to the northwest. The road ascends steadily. In about a mile, a very rough section must be negotiated. This backcountry obstacle course begins with a fallen tree, crosses an area washed out by a stream, and ascends a steep, rocky hill where it is advisable to take your skis off for the climb if any rocks show through the snow. Your reward for this considerable effort is entry into an area of backcountry which feels remote, though in fact it is not terribly far from the Junction Creek Road.

Having topped the steep, rocky hill, you are on a canyon edge with interesting views through the trees. Follow this edge for about a quarter of a mile, still ascending but at a reasonable grade for skiing. Look around for a fairly distinct road which drops down to your left and heads on the level through the woods to your right. Follow it to the right; in a while it will lead you past a substantial corral. The road is more distinct from this point on and leads you easily to the Junction Creek Road at a point 2.7 miles from the cattle guard back at the forest boundary.

You now have 800 feet of downhill at your disposal. If the snow cover on your ascent buried all the rocks, you might return as you came, bearing in mind that the steep hill will be an expert run or may have to be walked. If there were any spots of thin snow cover, you are better off descending the relatively smooth surface of the road, which can give you plenty of downhill fun. Be alert for snowmobiles as you rocket around the curves on the descent.　　　　　　　　　　　○

West from Durango to Cortez

In the Mancos Ranger District of the San Juan National Forest, varied ski touring opportunities exist within easy reach of Durango, Mancos, Cortez, Dolores, and northwestern New Mexico. On some forest roads in this area, there is a possibility that logging may occur in winter; call the Mancos District at 303 533-7716 or 303 385-1294 (Durango line) for current conditions.

O

6

La Plata Canyon Routes

Starting elevation: 8735 feet (2662 meters)
Maps: 7.5' La Plata
7.5' Hesperus
San Juan National Forest 1985 Travel Map

From Durango, it is 11 miles west on U.S. Highway 160 to the La Plata Canyon Road, which heads north at the Canyon Motel. The La Plata Canyon Road is plowed for the first 4 miles, to Mayday, where good parking for several cars is available at the end of the paved part of the road.

Snowmobile use on the canyon road is heavy, especially on weekends. Ski tourers can get off the road half a mile north of Mayday by cutting over to the right and skiing north along the riverbed. The river is covered by the snowpack in this deep mountain valley from December through March, and the river banks are sometimes skiable even longer. Skiers do have to return to the road after a mile and a half as the river's course becomes too rough to ski beyond this point. This first section of road and river skiing is suitable for beginners.

La Plata Canyon has several major snowslide paths which cross the road and others which come down to the riverbed. These present a hazard in times when natural releases are likely, and no part of the canyon should be skied when the overall avalanche danger for Colorado's southern mountains is rated high. Skiers passing through the runout zones at the bottom of these slidepaths are not likely to set off skier-caused snowslides in times of low avalanche danger, but caution should be exercised at all times.

Measuring mileages north from the Mayday parking spot: the first major slidepath crosses the road at 0.5 mile and another reaches the riverbed from the eastern wall of the canyon at about 1 mile. A third crosses the road at the Snowslide Gulch Recreational Area and a fourth just beyond at about 1.25 miles. These lie along the routes to Bedrock Creek and the Gold King Mill. Continuing on to the Tomahawk Basin

48

jeep road turnoff, four more major slidepaths cross the canyon road between 4.8 and 5.5 miles north of Mayday.

A
B E D R O C K   C R E E K

> **Distance:**   11 miles (17.7 kilometers) round trip
>   from Mayday
> **Elevation change:**   2100 feet (640 meters)
>   from Mayday
> **High point:**   10,835 feet (3303 meters)
> **Rating:**   Advanced
> **Time allowed:**   5 hours
> **Avalanche danger:**   Moderate - High

It is just under 3 miles north along the canyon road from the parking area at Mayday to the Bedrock Creek jeep road, which heads steeply uphill on the left just before the canyon road crosses Bedrock Creek. Climbing skins are recommended for the steep trip up the jeep road. The descent on this route is a fast, challenging shot. It should only be attempted by strong skiers with the ability to ski under control on steep, narrow downgrades.

The way up the jeep road is clear most of the time. Half a mile from the canyon road, the jeep road makes a sharp switchback. The grade beyond is steep at first, then moderates a bit. You traverse a clearing with a good view of Burwell Peak to the right as the route works its way up towards Gibbs peak. There is moderate avalanche danger along this section from a couple of slidepaths which cross the road.

At a point 1.7 miles up from the canyon road, where the jeep road makes a switchback, a spur road goes straight ahead to the Allard Mine. The ski route heads up the switchback. This is a steep section; coming back down this will be high-speed traversing, not fall-line

49

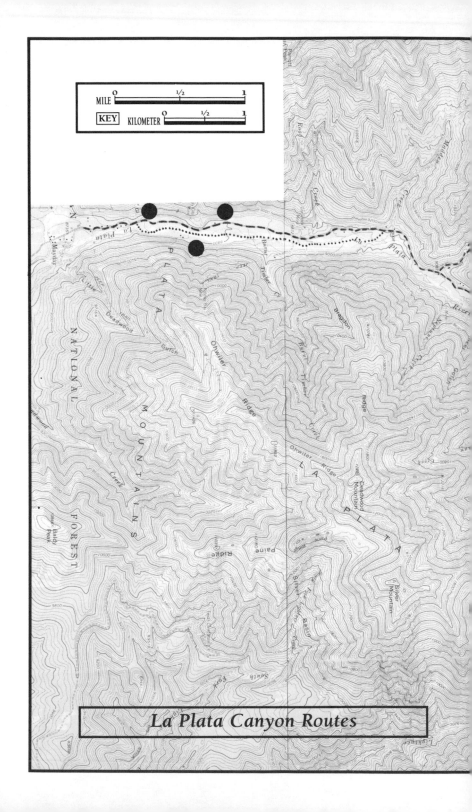

MILE 0 1/2 1

KEY KILOMETER 0 1/2 1

La Plata Canyon Routes

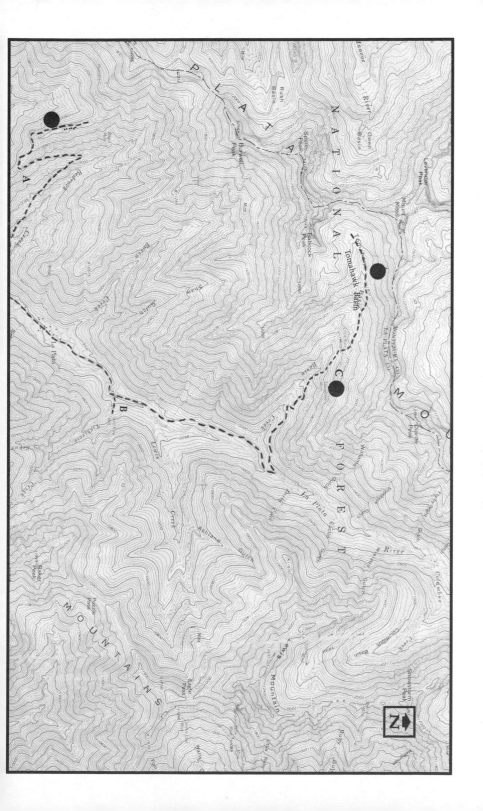

skiing. At the top of the slope, you round a turn and have a section at an easier grade. Avalanche danger increases beyond this.

Coming around to a west-facing slope, the flat path provided by the road will be filled in by snow, making your route a traverse across a steep slope. This area should not be skied in times of high avalanche danger, as it has the potential to be a starting zone for a snowslide which the skier could trigger.

If conditions are safe, traversing this section brings you to the top of a ridge where you are out of avalanche danger. A couple of hundred yards along the ridge brings you to the turnaround point, a clearing which affords a closer view of Burwell Peak. East of you, backtracking from the clearing, is a 10,880-foot knoll which can be climbed — with caution — for a panoramic view. The jeep road ahead to the west switchbacks up steep slopes on Gibbs Peak which presents extreme avalanche danger and should be considered unsafe at all times. Turning around, you descend over 1700 feet in the 2.5 miles back to the canyon road.

B

G O L D   K I N G   M I L L

> *Distance:*   9.5 miles (15.3 kilometers)
> *Elevation change:*   755 feet (230 meters) from
>   Mayday
> *Rating:*   Intermediate
> *Time allowed:*   6 hours
> *Avalanche danger:*   Moderate

Beyond Bedrock Creek, the canyon road reaches La Plata City about 3.5 miles north of Mayday. Once the residence of miners who worked claims in these mineral-rich mountains, the "city" now consists of a scattering of cabins in styles old and new.

A little under a mile north of La Plata City the canyon road

Gold King Mill.

Tour 6-B

traverses a rough, steep spot. Shortly beyond this there is a free-standing chimney (bound to topple eventually) which is the only remnant of a ruined building. From here, looking ahead and to the right, you can see the ruins of the Gold King Mill in the woods across the river. About 100 feet further on, ski down a short side road to the river bank and cross the river. The climb up the opposite bank is briefly steep and tricky.

Old roads lead you about a quarter of a mile uphill to the Gold King. Even in ruins, the structure is impressive. Since it is decaying, entering the mill building could be hazardous. The area outside the mill is an ideal lunch spot, however. When you leave, the descent back to the river is at a downhill grade which can be a fun run in good snow.

Tomahawk Basin; the ski route ascends the snowfields to right of center.
Tour 6-C

C
T O M A H A W K   B A S I N

Distance: 10.8 miles (17.3 kilometers) round trip
from La Plata City
Elevation change: 2140 feet (652 meters) from
canyon road
High point: 12,060 feet (3676 meters)
Rating: Advanced
Time allowed: 6 hours
Avalanche danger: High

A ski trip to Tomahawk Basin is primarily a spring tour for
advanced telemark skiers. Avalanche danger, too high for safe skiing
here most of the winter, is more predictable under spring conditions.
Access is also much easier when the canyon road has been plowed out
at least as far as La Plata City. This basin may still have good spring
skiing when the canyon road has been plowed all the way to the
Tomahawk Basin jeep road turnoff.

The turnoff from the canyon road is 5.9 miles north of Mayday and 2.5 miles north of La Plata City. The Tomahawk Basin jeep road is uphill on the left, beginning as a hairpin turn to the southwest from the canyon road. It crosses a rocky slope and then a snowslide path before coming into the open for good at a low treeline (10,400 feet) in about a mile. From here on, the rest of the route is in avalanche terrain.

The ascent should be made with a pre-dawn start on a clear morning in spring. Under such conditions, the snowpack will be frozen solid and will remain stable until the sun warms it. It may be possible to walk all the way up on top of the hard-frozen snowpack. If not, climbing skins are recommended.

From the point where the jeep road comes into the open, the route climbs steeply to the northwest. The upper basin is above and to the left. To reach it, stay north (to the right) of Basin Creek, gradually curving around to the west. You traverse up steep slopes until you are in the upper basin itself, where the grade moderates a bit. Here you are walled in by rugged peaks; start your descent and get out before the sun warms the snow enough to avalanche and the mountains show you how savage they really are.

○

Railroad Road

Distance: 8 miles (12.9 kilometers)
Starting elevation: 7960 feet (2426 meters)
Elevation change: 481 feet (147 meters)
High point: 8441 feet (2573 meters)
Rating: Novice - Intermediate
Time allowed: 6 hours
Avalanche danger: Low
Maps: 7.5' Thompson Park
             7.5' Hesperus

This route begins on the Madden Peak Road, which heads north from U.S. Highway 160 at the summit of Mancos Hill, 21.5 miles west of Durango and 5.6 miles east of Mancos. The ski tour ends at the Cherry Creek Picnic Ground on the northern side of Highway 160 at a point 16 miles west of Durango. You should park a second car on the roadside at the picnic area (gate closed in winter). There is another possibility for serious athletes: cache a bicycle at trail's end and turn this tour into a biathalon by biking the highway back to your car at the starting point.

The Madden Peak Road (Forest Road 316) will usually be plowed for the first quarter mile, to a point where a lumber yard is off to the left. From this spot, three-quarters of a mile of skiing along the road on an oak brush-covered plateau will bring you to the place where Forest Road 568, the Railroad Road, heads right. This is at the same spot as the clearing for a gas pipeline.

Taking the right onto the Railroad Road, you begin 6 miles of skiing which seems flat but in fact gains over 300 feet of elevation. You soon pass a gate and can see the road traversing the slope ahead. At first it makes a big curve, rounding the head of a stream drainage, then continues generally east. This route follows the grade of a former railroad which hauled coal from mines in this vicinity decades ago.

There is an option for a shorter tour which descends to Thompson Park Campground. About a mile beyond the gate, just beyond the second road cut which you pass through, a hiking trail heads downhill through the oak brush. There is a wooden post and a slight gap in the brush on the right at this point, but the trail may be quite obscure in winter conditions.

The first pitch down is the steepest and roughest; some walking may be in order here. The grade becomes more gentle and the trail is marked with blue paint blazes on trees when you get below the power line with steel lattice towers which you can see from the Railroad Road. Bear to the left of the power line tower which is most directly below the point where the trail starts down from the road. There are a couple of tight spots in the oak brush on the way to the campground, which you reach in less than a mile. It is then easy skiing on the campground loop roads to Highway 160 at a point 1.1 miles east of the summit of Mancos Hill.

The Thompson Park Campground loops by themselves make for a pleasant short tour for beginner and novice skiers. There is room to park a couple of cars at the campground entrance in front of the gate, which is closed in winter. This is 20.4 miles west of Durango on Highway 160. Intermediate skiers could also start here and ski the hiking trail up to the Railroad Road, taking off from campground site 37.

Continuing along the Railroad Road from the Thompson Park trail junction, it is 0.6 mile to "Aspen Pond," the first aspen grove you pass through. As bodies of water go, this one, adjacent to the road on the left, is either a tiny pond or a fair-sized puddle.

In the miles ahead, the road passes through an impressively deep road cut before reaching a bigger aspen grove at Starvation Creek, the largest stream which you cross. From Starvation Creek, it is about 1.7 miles to the Cherry Creek turnoff. A small sign with the number 2568 marks this road, which heads downhill to the right; watch for it, because the railroad grade does continue straight ahead at this point.

If all the flat skiing has left you starved for some downhill, the last mile of road down to Cherry Creek Picnic Ground will satisfy your appetite. It drops 480 feet. In deep, fresh snow novice skiers can handle it; faster snow conditions, more common here, make it an intermediate run. ○

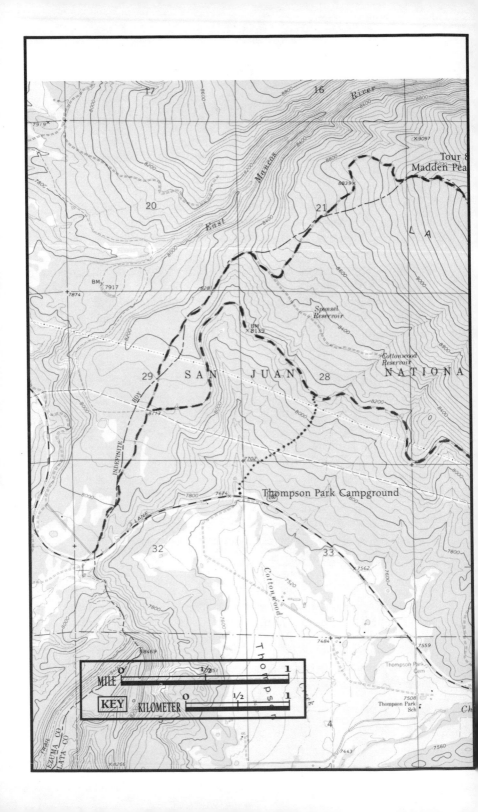

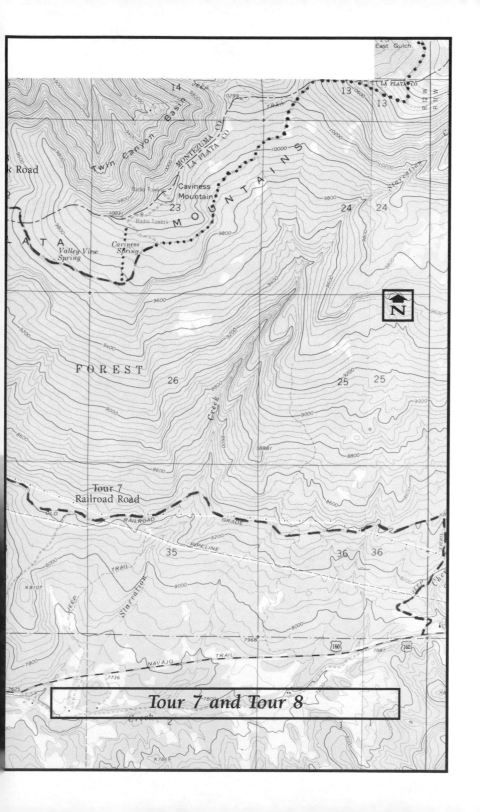

East Gulch

LA PLATA CO

R. 12 W
R. 11 W

JEEP

14

0299

13

13

TRAIL

Twin Canyon Basin

M
O
U
N
T
A
I
N
S

10000

10200

k Road

Radio Towers

Caviness
Mountain

23

24

24

M
O
U
N
T
A
I
N
S

10031

Radio Towers

Valley View
Spring

Caviness
Spring

9800

P L A T A

9600

Creek

9400

9200

N

9600

F O R E S T

26

8800

8881

25

25

9000

9400

9200

8800

9000

8600

8600

Tour 7
Railroad Road

RAILROAD

GRADE

8600

OLD

PIPELINE

TRAIL

35

8000

36

36

× 8107

TRAIL

JEEP

JEEP

Cher

Starvation

Starvation

8000

8000

7968

160

7897

160

7800

NAVAJO

TRAIL

7625

7736

Tour 7 and Tour 8

Creek

2

1

1

× 7865

8

Madden Peak Road

Distance: 11-16.5 miles (18-26 kilometers)
Starting elevation: 7960 feet (2426 meters)
Elevation change: 2040-3080 feet
  (622-939 meters)
High point: 10,000-11,040 feet
  (3048-3365 meters)
Rating: Intermediate - Advanced
Time allowed: 6-8 hours
Avalanche danger: Low - Moderate
Maps: 7.5' Thompson Park
  7.5' Hesperus
  7.5' La Plata

The Madden Peak Road heads north from U.S. Highway 160 at the summit of Mancos Hill, 5.6 miles east of Mancos (21.5 miles west of Durango). It will usually be plowed for the first quarter mile, to a point where a lumberyard is off to the left. Park and start skiing from here.

Three-quarters of a mile in, Forest Road 568 (Railroad Road) goes off to the right. Continue straight ahead on the Madden Peak Road. After 2 miles of flat skiing you begin to gain elevation. A side road to two reservoirs branches off to the right at 2.25 miles; this might make an interesting side trip.

Continuing steadily uphill, the road crosses a cattle guard 3.25 miles from your starting point. Not long after this, aspen groves begin to replace pine forests as you climb into a cooler, moister climactic zone. These aspen forests are popular with loggers, as you see in the next 2 miles; much of this area has been cut over. At about 5 miles from your starting point, one of the logging cuts affords you a good view to the south.

Half a mile further on, a power line which goes up to a group of radio towers crosses the road. The towers crown the summit of 10,031-foot Caviness Mountain. The clearing under the power line has the potential for some downhill fun, bearing in mind a few cautions.

Snowcats accasionally ascend this cleared path for access to the electronic site (the radio towers) above; be alert for them and be aware that their tracks may affect ski conditions. The public is requested to stay off of the electronic site itself. You can ski up the power line clearing, but should turn around before entering the area immediately around the radio towers, which does not offer anything exciting to the skier in any case.

When you ski back down, you can continue to follow the power line to a point below where it crosses the road, but plan on climbing back up. The clearing provides a good run as long as it is in the aspen, but if you go too far down you will get into miles of troublesome oak brush. After skiing nearly 6 miles just to get here, you may not have the energy for a long climb up if you descend too far.

The power line crossing is the turnaround point for the shorter mileage tour given in the heading. The longer mileage and greater elevation gain are for a tour which continues all the way to the end of the Madden Peak Road. Due to its length and steeper grades, the longer tour is recommended only for strong intermediate and advanced skiers.

From the power line, the Madden Peak Road continues to ascend at a gentle grade. In half a mile, a vehicle access road to the electronic site branches off to the left; skiers should stay off of it. Madden Peak Road continues ahead and becomes more primitive; be alert for areas of potential avalanche danger from here to the road's end. The route drops slightly, then climbs much more steeply, continuing into the backcountry and dead-ending on the western slope of Madden Peak 2.5 miles beyond the electronic site road turnoff. The road passes over its high point, 11,040 feet, a bit before dropping to its dead end. Getting all the way to the end and back is a marathon tour.

○

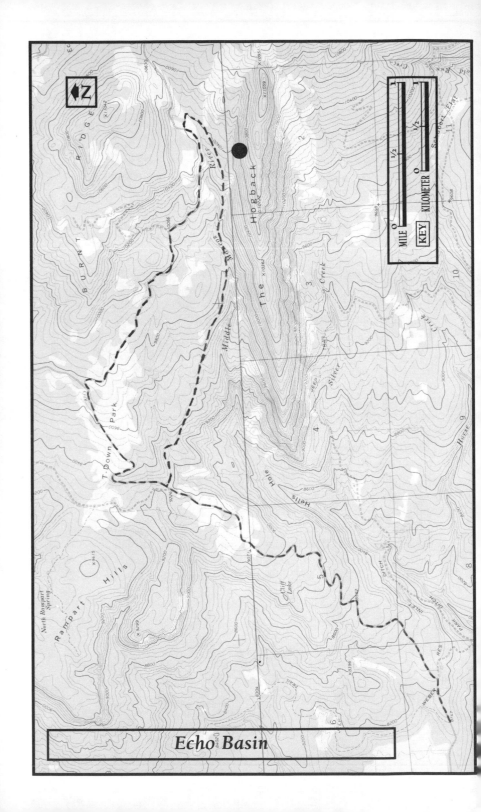

Echo Basin

9

Echo Basin

Distance: 9-13 miles (14-21 kilometers)
Starting elevation: 8150 feet (2484 meters)
Elevation change: 1560-2250 feet
   (475-686 meters)
High point: 9713-10,400 feet
   (2960-3170 meters)
Rating: Intermediate - Advanced
Time allowed: 6-8 hours
Avalanche danger: Low - Moderate
Maps: 7.5' Rampart Hills
      San Juan National Forest 1985 Travel Map

For the skier with lots of endurance, the Echo Basin Road provides a chance to tour all the way from the ponderosa pine zone to the boreal forest on the western flank of the La Platas. The road accesses a large area of attractive backcountry with opportunities for many medium to long trips. Destinations include wintry playgrounds for intermediate skiers in open meadows and an interesting telemarking run for more advanced skiers.

The Echo Basin Road heads north from U.S. Highway 160 at a point 2.5 miles east of Mancos and 24.5 miles west of Durango. The pavement ends 2.4 miles in from Highway 160, but the dirt road should be plowed for another mile because there are residences along it. The San Juan National Forest boundary is crossed at a cattle guard 3.3 miles from Highway 160. Park and start skiing from wherever the plowing stops. This will probably be at the South Rampart Road (Forest Road 328) junction, 0.25 mile beyond the forest boundary.

Ski straight ahead up Forest Road 566, the Echo Basin Road. After a short flat section beneath ponderosa pines, the road begins a relentless climb for the next 3 miles. It makes several switchbacks as it ascends at a grade which is not steep but is sustained. Take it at your best pace for an aerobic workout second to none.

As you near the top of the oak brush ascent, a view of the cliffs of the Rampart Hills opens up on your left. A quarter mile beyond this you cross a cattle guard (the second since the start of the ascent) and come to an open meadow where oak brush at last gives way to aspen. The evergreen-forested ridge of the Hogback is on your right; turn towards it to find the spot where the road descends briefly from the meadow to a low spot between hills where three roads diverge.

There is quite a maze of roads in the area ahead. No map shows all of them; the San Juan National Forest 1985 Travel Map comes closest. The Rampart Hills quad shows the main Echo Basin Road, which makes a big loop, but not any of the numerous side roads. At the low spot between hills, the Box Canyon Road (Forest Road 331) goes left and slightly downhill, the Echo Basin Road — your ski route — is seen ahead climbing to the left (west) up the next hillside, and a third road goes off to the right around the other side (east) of the same hill.

Telemarkers take note: this third road is the route down from the "Hogback Run," the telemarking tour whose upper end is best reached by continuing up the eastern side of the main Echo Basin loop road. For clarity I will call it the "Hogback Road" since it is the road which stays closest to the Hogback.

Continuing up the Echo Basin Road (the middle of the three) from the triple junction, the route makes a switchback to the right, another turn to the left, and enters an open meadow. Here the road vanishes beneath the snowpack, but it continues in the same direction and enters aspen forest where the way is clear again. Turn around here and admire the wide views of Mesa Verde and distant mountains in Utah and Arizona.

After passing through about a half mile of aspen, the road emerges in another meadow. This is T-Down Park, where the Echo Basin Road forks. There is a sign here, but the snow may be deep enough to bury it. This point is about 1 mile from the triple junction.

This is the turnaround point for the 9-mile tour for intermediate skiers. T-Down park is your winter playground; climb and descend its slopes as much as your energy permits. You need go no further than this, on a sunny winter day with wide views, to have earned the feeling

Helmet Peak from the Echo Basin Road.

that you have climbed above the world of the ordinary.

Strong intermediates and telemark skiers can continue on the 13-mile tour which includes the Hogback Run. Take the right (east) branch of the Echo Basin loop road, which heads across T-Down Park towards Helmet Peak. You skirt the edge of the aspen forest for a while, then enter woods of 25-foot trees. You cross a cattle guard and pass a rockpile on your left. Forest Road 337 branches off to the left after these. Continuing uphill in the aspen, stay left where a side road branches off to the right.

Farther on, the ruins of the Guymon cabin are on a flat below the road to the right; they may not be obvious in deep snow. The stream in the gully below and to the right at this point is the Middle Mancos River. Your downhill return trip is on the other side of the river, which can be easily crossed farther up. Keep an eye on the terrain to your right to find the crossing.

After you have ascended into spruce-fir forest, there will be lightly wooded and fairly flat country to your right. Forest Road 566H, primitive and more obscure than the main road that you have been following, branches off to the right in an area where your long climb has at last, more or less, levelled out. There is a small signpost, but it may be out of sight beneath the snow. This is deep backcountry where finding the route is a matter of your own skill, not of artificial aid. Here you can easily cross the head of the stream — no steep gully climbing is involved. This point is 2.25 miles from the fork in the road at T-Down Park.

A broad U-turn brings you around the head of the stream and towards the western side of the Hogback near its upper end. Steep slopes on the Hogback present a significant avalanche hazard; this route should not be skied in times of high avalanche danger.

Between the Hogback and the Middle Mancos River, the slope I call the Hogback Run leads you down between widely spaced trees for a mile. It is a steeper way down than the route you have ascended, but its ample width, openness, and favorable aspect for good snow conditions make it suitable for telemarkers of all ability levels. At the bottom of the run you pick up a fairly distinct logging road for the last couple of hundred yards and cross the snow-bridged stream.

The Hogback Road leads downhill from this point at a less steep grade. Follow it for a bit less than 2 miles back to the triple junction. Be alert for a washout which has taken out a 30-foot section of the road a mile or so down.

The full Echo Basin loop, which you departed from to take the Hogback Run, is 9 miles around. With the additional 9-mile round trip from the trailhead to T-Down Park, it would make for an 18-mile tour. Skiers who happen to be marathon runners could do it as a day trip, but for mere mortals it would be better to plan it as a winter backpack. The Echo Basin area is an attractive one for this.

○

Mesa Verde National Park ∘ Cortez, Colorado

Distance: 6 miles (10 kilometers)
Starting elevation: 7040 feet (2146 meters)
Elevation change: Down 200 feet (61 meters) and
   back up
Rating: Beginner
Time allowed: 3 hours
Park telephone: 303 529-4461
Maps: 7.5' Moccasin Mesa
   Mesa Verde National Park (topographic)

The eastern loop of the Ruins Road at Mesa Verde is not plowed. During most winters, it has enough snow for skiing occasionally for a few days just after snowstorms. Call the park to check on conditions. The main park access road is kept open all winter; there is a park entrance fee of $5 per vehicle.

The park entrance is 8 miles east of Cortez and 36 miles west of Durango on U.S. Highway 160. It is a 20-mile drive along the winding park access road to the point where the Ruins Road heads off to the left. The park museum is to the right from this intersection. There is a gate here; if it is closed, park at the roadside but do not block the gate in case of a need for emergency access by park personnel.

If this gate is closed and the western loop of the Ruins Road has not been plowed, you may be able to ski on both loops. The park plows out the western loop for automobile access, but there may be times just after snowstorms when it has not yet been plowed. The eastern loop is never plowed (though as mentioned above, snow deep enough for skiing is only intermittent on the mesa).

Half a mile from the gate, the Ruins Road forks. The western loop goes straight ahead; the eastern loop, the usual ski route, goes off to the left.

The eastern loop makes a 5.7-mile circuit on the Balcony House Road. At a point 1.3 miles from the first fork, the road makes a second fork where its loop begins and ends. It is 3.1 miles around the loop,

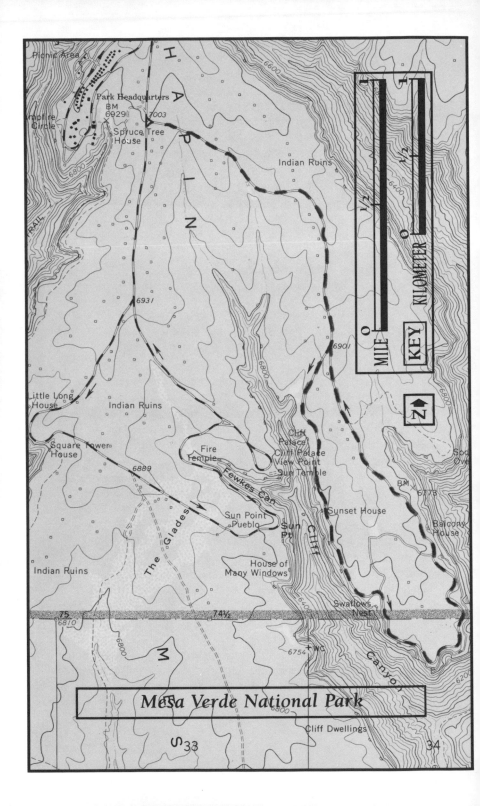

Mesa Verde National Park

*Linda Faldetta at the Cliff Palace Viewpoint on the western loop
of the Ruins Road.*

which passes by the trailheads to Cliff Palace and Balcony House.
These trails and the cliff dwellings themselves are closed to public
access in winter. There are views across the canyon to other ruins,
however.

The western loop, whether you do it in your car or on skis, makes
a 5.3-mile circuit. Three-quarters of a mile from where the eastern loop
branches off to the left, the road forks again; this is the beginning and
end of the loop on the western side. Going right here leads you to the
Navajo Canyon Overlook in three-quarters of a mile, Sun Point in 2
miles, and the short side road to the Cliff Palace Viewpoint in a bit
under 3 miles. Mesa-top ruins exhibits are located along the way. From
the Cliff Palace spur road, it is 0.6 mile back to the end of the loop,
where you bear right for the return. At times when both loops can be
skied, ambitious skiers doing both can go a total of 12 miles.

Whichever way you choose, the pinyon-juniper forest of Mesa
Verde surrounds you most of the way. The sharp spines of yucca poke
up through the snow and rabbitbrush may be decorated with frost.
There are subtle earth tone colors in the plants of this semi-desert
environment during their winter dormancy.

At viewpoints the larger-scale drama of sandstone canyons and

Anasazi ruins becomes evident. The combination of ski touring and archeology here is a unique experience; one wonders what the Ancient Ones would have thought of cross-country skis. I would guess that they had one thing in common with skiers; a liking for snow, which augmented their supply of life-sustaining water. In contrast to driving this road in its busy summer season, skiing the Ruins Road brings the skier closer to the primeval silence of the canyons. It also sets a pace more like that of the ancient rhythm of the Anasazi themselves.

The park provides two other possibilities for ski touring. Both are located on the higher-elevation northern end of the mesa, where they can have good snow even when the Ruins Road loops are not skiable. The Point Lookout quadrangle topographic map shows these two areas.

One is the Morfield Campground, to the right of the park access road 4 miles from the park entrance. Skiing is on gently rolling terrain in oak brush. An easy tour of a mile or so can be made by following the campground roads, which meander and loop around.

The second is a longer tour down Prater Canyon. You must notify the park office by telephone when you plan to ski this route; otherwise, your car parked at the roadside will be taken as an indication of an emergency and park police will be out looking for you.

On your way into the park, just after passing Morfield Campground, you drive through a tunnel. There is a wide space just on the other side of it for parking. Ski south from the park road down the canyon; a round-trip tour of 6 miles is possible, descending 400 feet and then returning. The southernmost portion of this tour is on the Moccasin Mesa quad. ○

Additional Area — *West from Durango to Cortez*

H E S P E R U S   S K I   A R E A

This area is located on the southern side of U.S. Highway 160 just west of La Plata Canyon Road, about 12.5 miles west of Durango (26 miles east of Cortez). A groomed 10-kilometer loop trail for Nordic skiers begins at the base area and heads west, staying on a north-facing slope. The trail fee is $2.50; for information call 303 247-3711. ○

North from Durango to Silverton

A sampling of everything southwestern Colorado has to offer the cross-country skier can be found along the corridor from Durango north to Silverton. There are trails in a variety of terrain types for skiers at each level of ability. Some areas offer skiing which is free from avalanche danger; others hold steep downhill challenges for advanced skiers with the usual accompanying avalanche hazards. There are even the groomed trails of the Purgatory Nordic Center, and the Purgatory downhill ski area which welcomes telemarkers.

Mileages north from Durango along U.S. Highway 550 are measured from the intersection of 32nd Street and Main Avenue. For the distance south from Silverton, take the mileage north from Durango and subtract it from 47 miles.

Ski routes in this area are in the Animas Ranger District of the San Juan National Forest. Offices are located in the Federal Building at 701 Camino del Rio in Durango, telephone 303 247-4874.

○

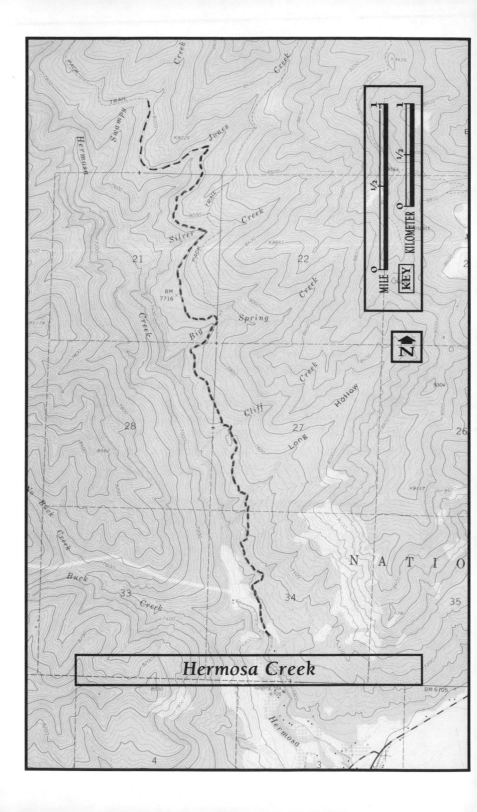

KEY

MILE

0   1/2   1/2   1

KILOMETER

0   1/2   1/2   1

N

Hermosa Creek

Hermosa Creek

Distance: 6-8 miles (10-13 kilometers)
Starting elevation: 6780 feet (2067 meters)
Elevation change: 980-1170 feet (299-357 meters)
Rating: Beginner - Intermediate
Time allowed: 3-5 hours
Avalanche danger: Low
Map: 7.5' Hermosa

Hermosa, "beautiful" in Spanish, is a name which has become attached to several geographic features north of Durango. The Hermosa Cliffs parallel U.S. Highway 550 on the west for several miles around Purgatory. Hermosa Creek flows out of the hills to join the Animas River south of this, near the village of Hermosa, a little over 8 miles from the northern end of Durango on Highway 550. Head west here at the sign for the Hermosa Creek Road, then take a quick right and drive up the hill to the starting point for this ski tour. Park where snow plowing stops, usually at a cattle guard beyond the last of a few driveways leading to residences.

Skiing ahead up the unplowed road, it is 0.7 mile to the national forest boundary. One-quarter mile beyond this, you pass a corral on the right. The grade is uphill all the way, but never particularly steep. Gambel oak and ponderosa pine line the road, which has interesting views of cliffs and the canyon of Hermosa Creek which flows far below to the left.

From a point 1.7 miles beyond the national forest boundary to the end of the road at 2.2 miles, the land on both sides of the road is private property where "No Trespassing" is posted. Skiers should avoid taking any side trips off the road here; there is ample terrain for exploration ahead on public land.

The shorter tour listed in the heading presumes a trip to the end of the road and back. This is an easy route suitable for beginner and novice skiers. Continuing ahead on the Hermosa Trail is too rough for first-time skiers, but novices with some experience under their belts might attempt it. Bear in mind that it may be difficult at points for skiers of less than intermediate ability.

The longer tour described in the heading continues 1.1 miles on the Hermosa trail to Swampy Creek. This additional distance is likely to take you as long as the preceding 3 miles on the road due to the rougher terrain. For your effort, you are rewarded with a sense of really being in the backcountry where nature's work is far more prominent than that of man.

The trail starts with a short downhill pitch which novice skiers will find intimidating under all but the slowest snow conditions. If you really have trouble negotiating this, do not continue; there is a longer stretch of equal difficulty ahead.

The Hermosa Trail rounds the drainage of Silver Creek and climbs out to a gambel oak slope with a view of the big canyon of Hermosa Creek. The trail then descends as it rounds the gulch of Jones Creek; this drop is the difficult one mentioned above, a longer downgrade on the narrow trail than anything which has preceded it. After crossing Jones Creek, you ascend out of its drainage; this is the pattern of the Hermosa Trail for many miles ahead. You ski through a beautiful grove of red-trunked ponderosa pines not long before reaching Swampy Creek, which has a trail bridge over it.

Turning back from here gives you a tour with a nice taste of the backcountry. On the trip back down the road, the grade is such that waxable skis have a chance to demonstrate that they glide better than waxless skis. The fish scales or mohair on the bases of waxless skis slow you down on a gentle descent; of course if the wax on your waxable skis is too sticky for the snow conditions, you can have the same problem.

○

Haviland Lake Routes

Starting elevation: 8165 feet (2489 meters)
Avalanche danger: Low
Map: 7.5' Electra Lake

The Haviland Lake Road heads east from U.S. Highway 550 just over 17 miles from the northern end of Durango. It gives access to a ski touring area with several options for beginner to intermediate skiers. There is space for parking several cars off of the highway here. Just north of the Haviland Lake Road on the same side of the highway is Bear Ranch, where trails formerly maintained as a touring center can be skied by skiers of all ability levels.

This area is good during stormy periods when the avalanche danger is too high to ski safely in higher-elevation areas. On the other hand, snow conditions on south-facing slopes here are rather poor during long periods without snow. The best skiing conditions occur in January and February and just after snowstorms in December and March.

A

A S P E N   G R O V E S   L O O P

Distance: 2 miles (3.2 kilometers)
Elevation change: Down 100 feet and back up
Rating: Novice - Intermediate
Time allowed: 1.5 hours

This blazed trail leaves the Haviland Lake Road on the right 0.2 mile from the highway, just before the intersection with the road down to Chris Park. The blazes are small square blue signs marked "X-C." The trail is a loop which can be skied in either direction; I prefer taking the left branch for the descent. The fork in the trail

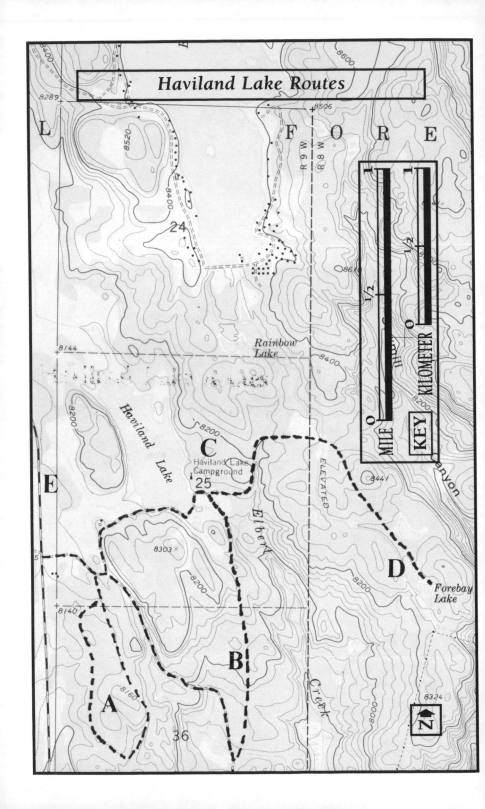

where the loop begins and ends is just a short distance from the point where the trail leaves the road.

Taking the left fork, you ski through a forest of ponderosa pine, Douglas fir, and Rocky Mountain juniper along a minor ridge. There are a couple of descents which will be challenging for novices in fast snow conditions. The trail descends to the right through an aspen grove and continues through aspen on the flat. There is a small hill climb — again, challenging for novices — and then a gentler ascent winding through the woods back to the trailhead.

B

ANIMAS - SILVERTON WAGON ROAD

> **Distance:**   3 miles (4.8 kilometers)
> **Elevation change:**   Down 300 feet (91.4 meters)
>   and back up
> **Rating:**   Intermediate
> **Time allowed:**   2.5 hours

This primitive old road, which has been blazed recently for skiing, takes you along a historic route where ox-drawn wagons and horse-drawn stages travelled over a hundred years ago. I recommend skiing the trail down and coming back up the Chris Park Road. This makes for downhill fun in a backcountry setting and an easy ascent on the return.

Follow the Haviland Lake Road around the southern shore of the lake to the campground entrance, 0.8 miles from the highway. The trail leaves the road on the right just below a jeep road which heads off into the woods. Check snow conditions on southern exposures as you start down the trail. Much of the descent below is on rocky south-facing slopes which need good snow cover to be worth doing. The trail descends through open pines at first, then crosses Elbert Creek and descends through thicker woods. There is a bit of ascent on a north-facing slope. After this it is almost all downhill; the grade at points gets steep enough for some fast skiing.

The Chris Park Road and picnic area will be on the right when you reach the bottom of the descent. There is a sign explaining the history of the wagon road here. It is 0.8 mile back up the road to the junction with the Haviland Lake Road, where you take a left and go 0.2 mile to return to your car.

C
H A V I L A N D   L A K E   C A M P G R O U N D

> ***Distance:***   2.2 miles (3.5 kilometers)
> ***Elevation change:***   Up 80 feet (24 meters)
>   and back down
> ***Rating:***   Beginner - Novice
> ***Time allowed:***   2 hours

The campground loop road makes a pleasant tour suitable for first-time skiers. Ski the Haviland Lake Road, taking a left at the intersection with the Chris Park Road and continuing around the southern shore of the lake to the campground entrance 0.8 mile from the highway. The distance around the campground loop is 0.6 mile. Taking the right side of the loop first gives you a bit of climbing followed by some descent, all at gentle grades.

*Along the
Animas-Silverton
Wagon Road.*

Tour 12-C

D

F O R E B A Y   L A K E

Distance: 4 miles (6.4 kilometers)
Elevation change: Up 210 feet (64 meters),
   down 260 feet (79 meters), then back
Rating: Intermediate
Time allowed: 3 hours

Follow the Haviland Lake Road around the southern shore of the
lake to the campground. Ski off to the right on a jeep road which
heads into the woods from the start of the campground loop road. The

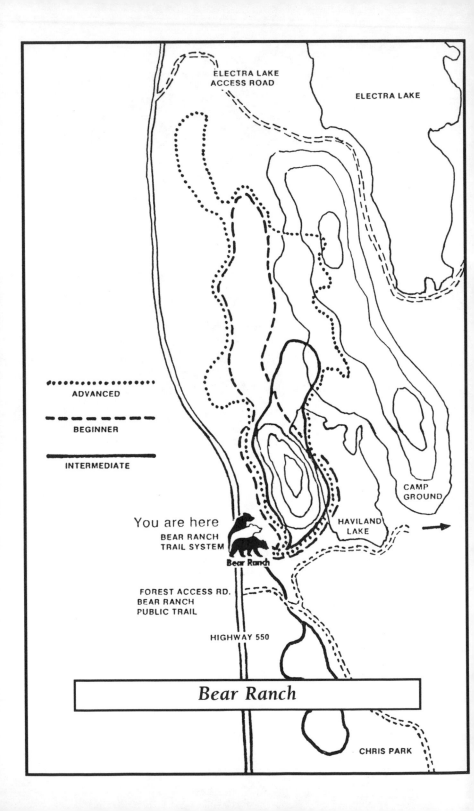

jeep road makes a curve to the left and climbs a hill not far from the start. It then makes a sharp right to cross a stream and climbs steeply up the other side. After this it bears right again.

Coming into the open, you see a big pipeline ahead and join another road. Bear right again here. The road crosses under the pipe and climbs to the high point of the tour, then descends. Rolling terrain leads you to Forebay Lake, somewhat over a mile from the campground area and 50 feet lower in elevation than your starting point back at the highway. This is a good spot for a winter picnic before a leisurely tour back.

BEAR RANCH

42570 Highway 550
Durango, Colorado 81301
303 247-0111

Distance: Up to 9.5 miles (15 kilometers)
Rating: Novice - Advanced

The ski trails at Bear Ranch were formerly maintained as a ski touring center, but the trails are not groomed here at present. Skiers can park at the ranch and tour the area, making their own tracks, at no charge. All trails start by heading around the southern end of the hill just beyond the ranch buildings and then turning north along the western shore of Haviland Lake. At the northern end of the lake, novice, intermediate, and advanced routes diverge.

The advanced route — the "Macho Man" loop — is about 15 kilometers with many ups and downs including a half-mile downhill run. It works its way to the north almost to the Electra Lake Road, then loops around to the west. On the way back it comes south down

81

the valley, roughly paralleling Highway 550. Bear Ranch offers bed and breakfast accommodations, restaurant and bar service, and a hot tub which can be rented by the hour (check for availability).

O

Purgatory Ski Touring Center

Post Office Box 666
Durango, Colorado 81302
303 247-9000

Maintained tracks for all ability levels
Distance: 9.5 miles (15 kilometers)
Starting elevation: 8700 feet (2652 meters)
Trail fee: $4
Equipment rental: $10/day; $6/half day (12:30 pm)
Trail map: Available at touring center

The touring center at Purgatory Ski Area is located on the eastern side of U.S. Highway 550 one-quarter mile north of the main entrance road to the downhill area. Trails starting here wind through the aspen forest on a plateau between the slopes of the alpine ski area to the

View from the Bench Trail.

west and a drop to the Lime Creek watershed on the east. Tracks suitable for both touring and skating are set. Individual and group lessons are available.

A short beginner's loop circumnavigates Twilight Lake south of the touring center building. The longer trails are to the north. The Bench Loop (intermediate) offers a good view of Spud Mountain and the Twilight Peaks. The only really steep pitch is on the black diamond Deadman's Loop; it is a straight shot which drops about fifty feet down a hillside, with ample room at the bottom for a runout. The terrain is predominantly intermediate in character, with moderate vertical relief providing enough ups and downs to make for enjoyable skiing.

At the downhill ski area, Purgatory has offered monthly telemark clinics for the past few years. The price for a group lesson and lift ticket has been just half the regular cost of an all-day lift ticket. Call or write for current status and a schedule.

O

14

Cascade Creek

Distance: 4-7 miles (6.4-11 kilometers)
Starting elevation: 8760 feet (2670 meters)
Elevation change: 440 feet (134 meters)
Rating: Novice - Intermediate
Time allowed: 3-5 hours
Avalanche danger: Low
Map: 7.5' Engineer Mountain

From Durango, it is 26.5 miles north on U.S. Highway 550 to the first hairpin turn which begins the climb to Coalbank Pass. This is 3.2 miles north of the Purgatory Ski Area entrance. On the right there is a large parking area; the Cascade Creek Road is across the highway.

The Cascade Creek Road leads you northwest with the creek on your left. The grade is quite gentle for the first mile, after which you pass cabins on the right and make a short steep climb up to a bridge over a wooden aqueduct. The uphill grade is steeper and the road more primitive for the next mile; you continue to pass cabins off in the woods to the right. At an apparent fork in the road, stay left.

The forest is very attractive here. Aspen is dominant, with blue spruce and Douglas fir in wetter areas. Blue columbine, state flower of Colorado, blooms profusely here in June. It is something worth contemplating when skiing Cascade Creek in a blizzard in January.

After passing through a gate (left open in winter), you cross a clearing where the last of the cabins is on the right. The road narrows. Ahead, at a spot with an uphill opening in the woods on the right, there is a fork in the route. There are almost always snowmobile tracks heading both ways. The left fork leads you on the longer tour described in the heading; continuing straight ahead leads you on the shorter option.

Proceeding straight ahead from the fork, you will reach the end of the road at the head of the summer hiking trail up Cascade Creek. The summer trail goes on, but is an extremely rough route in winter on a southern slope where the snow cover can be very poor at points. At

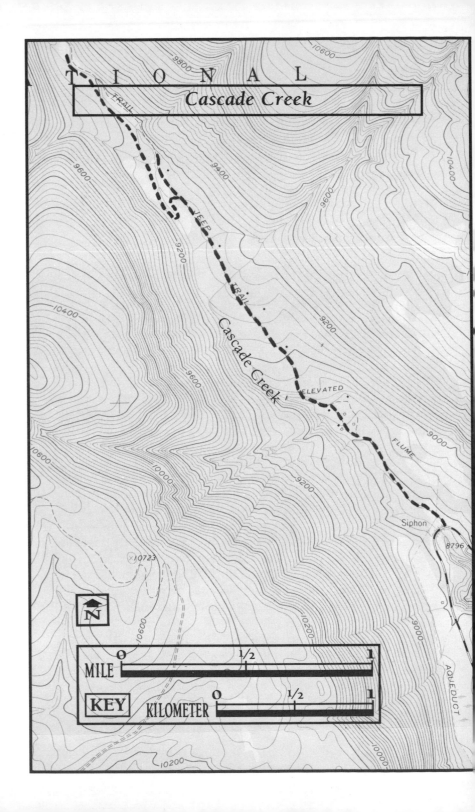

Cascade Creek

Glenn McGeoch descending the Cascade Creek Road.

the end of the road you are right next to the creek, which is big enough that open water flows all winter. Turning back from here gives you a fine tour with an exhilarating downhill grade; on fast old snow, novices will find it quite challenging.

Taking the left route from the fork, you soon round a turn and double back briefly in the downstream direction along the creek. This leads you to a bridge, which you cross and then resume your upstream heading on the other side of the creek. The route passes through a clearing which it exits towards the right-hand side, then continues through thick evergreen woods. In half a mile, you reach another clearing which has a six-foot-high "stairstep" running across it. Snow-mobilers frolic here, making tracks all over the place.

Beyond this clearing, the route may be harder to find, depending on whether other skiers or snowmobilers have left you a trail. The way continues between the creek and the steep slope on your left, getting narrower and rougher from here to Pando Creek, the turnaround point for this longer tour. In your favor as you forge ahead into more rugged backcountry is the fact that snow conditions on this northern slope are generally quite good.

About a half mile of the bumpy and heavily forested terrain traversed by the trail brings you to Pando Creek. A sign on a tree identifies the creek. The trail goes on from here, continuing in rough backcountry with some gentler sections, but this makes a good turn-around point.

On the return trip from either fork, the descent back down the road is one of the most enjoyable cross-country downhill runs around. It can be handled by reasonably fit novice skiers with the strength for some sustained snowplowing; it is an excellent place to practice the half-snowplow or "feather" turn. Do be alert for snowmobiles coming up the road.

Snowmobile use, alas, is quite heavy at Cascade Creek. Commercial snowmobile tours use this as a route. Weekdays are best for avoiding the machines.

O

15

Old Lime Creek Road

Distance: 10.5 miles (17 kilometers) one way
Starting elevation: 9776 feet (2980 meters)
Elevation change: Down 1400 feet (427 meters),
    up 500 feet (152 meters)
Rating: Intermediate
Time allowed: 5 hours
Avalanche danger: Moderate
Maps: San Juan County (topographic)
    7.5' Engineer Mountain
    7.5' Snowdon Peak

The historic Old Lime Creek Road was part of the route from
Durango to Silverton in horse-drawn wagon days, long before U.S.
Highway 550 was built over Coalbank Pass. Now part of the San Juan
National Forest (Forest Road 591), the road provides a ski route with
unique views of the West Needles Range. Along the way, the 13,000-
foot Twilight Peaks rise abruptly from the eastern side of the deep
canyon of Lime Creek. Dramatic ice falls decorate the steep, rocky
flank of Spud Mountain on the canyon's western side. At the end of
this tour, the skier can look back at the impressive ridgeline of the
West Needles Range knowing that he or she has just traversed its entire
length, albeit on a gently sloping route at the base of the peaks.

The starting point for this tour is 3 miles north of the summit of
Coalbank Pass on U.S. Highway 550, before the road begins its climb
to Molas Pass. This point is 35 miles north of Durango and 12 miles
south of Silverton. There is a sign for "Old Lime Creek Road" on the
eastern side of the highway, though the road itself may not be obvious
behind the snowbank left by highway plowing. Parking is limited,
especially during or shortly after snowstorms when highway crews
have not had time to clear the shoulder.

The distance and time given above assume a one-way trip on the
Old Lime Creek Road, which requires spotting a second car at the
lower end. Ample parking is available there at the hairpin turn where

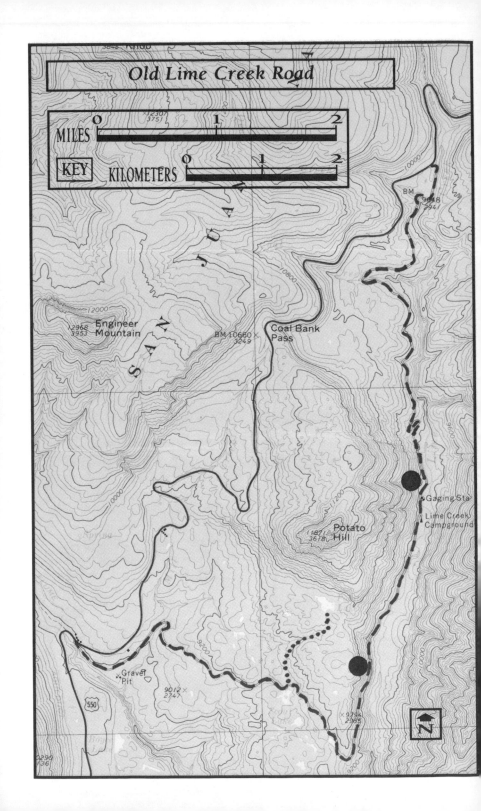

Ice fall and North Twilight Peak from the Old Lime Creek Road.

U.S. Highway 550 begins the climb to Coalbank Pass, 0.4 mile north of Cascade Village (29 miles north of Durango). This is the same parking area used for skiing Cascade Creek. After dropping a car off there, it is an 8.3-mile drive over Coalbank Pass to the upper end of the Old Lime Creek Road where this tour begins.

The Old Lime Creek Road descends very gently at the start. After crossing a bridge over Coal Creek, the road rises to the highest point of the tour, 9803 feet, at about the one mile point. Lime Creek is below and to the left. North Twilight Peak, straight ahead, dominates the more distant view.

In the next 3 miles the road descends 700 feet to the level of Lime Creek. Near the bottom, there are a couple of hairpin turns. The time estimate given for this tour assumes that you will be able to move at double-poling speed or better on the steeper portions of this descent. If you find yourself breaking trail in deep, fresh snow, your progress could be sunstantially slower.

Shortly after reaching the floor of Lime Creek Canyon, 4 miles from the start, the road crosses the runout zone of a major snowslide path. This area presents a hazard during heavy snowfall or within 48 hours afterward. My advice is not to ski this portion of the route when avalanche danger for Colorado's southern mountains is rated high.

After crossing the slidepath, the road follows the flat bottom of Lime Creek Canyon and within a mile brings you to the location of the former Lime Creek Campground. While not a maintained campground any longer, it is still a popular place in summer, in contrast to the quiet solitude you are likely to find there in winter. This is a logical lunch or rest stop. With the picturesque creek near at hand and the peaks towering above, it is a place you may want to linger.

Going on from the campground site, the road ascends 500 feet in 2 miles, traversing a steep slope at the stiffest uphill grade which you will encounter on the whole tour. About two-thirds of the way up, a second major avalanche path crosses the road; several smaller snowslide paths are also evident along this section. As the road climbs, the views open up. It includes a look at the bottom of an avalanche path on the other side of the canyon where foot-thick aspen trunks lie scattered about like matchsticks.

The road continues uphill around a bend which takes you away from the view and into aspen forest. Within half a mile you top out; it is almost all downhill from here to the place where you spotted your second car at road's end, about 4 miles away. The first downhill pitch is a little less than a mile long. It ends at a white opening in the woods which in summer is revealed as a swamp made by beaver activity.

The hiking trail to Spud Lake heads north from this spot. It provides an interesting side trip if time permits. The trail leads uphill 1 mile over terrain which is rough and steep for skiing. Just before reaching the lake, the route is somewhat obscure; the trail rounds the right side of a little beaver pond and continues north. The lake ("Potato

Lake" on USGS maps) sits in a wild and beautiful spot at the foot of rocky Spud Mountain ("Potato Hill" on USGS maps). This side trip involves 440 feet of additional elevation gain. The return trip is down the same trail.

From the Spud Lake Trail junction, Old Lime Creek Road descends to the west. Snowmobile use, light at the upper end of the road, becomes heavier here, especially towards the end where several cabins are located. A little while after crossing an open field you will reach the parking area at U.S. Highway 550 north of Cascade Village.

For a shorter tour — and one which is safe in times of high avalanche danger — it is possible to simply ski in from this lower end of the road. This also has the advantage of not requiring two cars. Avalanche danger is low all the way to Spud Lake, or to the topping-out point before the big drop into Lime Creek Canyon from this direction. Either choice is an 8-mile round trip with 800 feet of elevation change (uphill going in, downhill coming out).

O

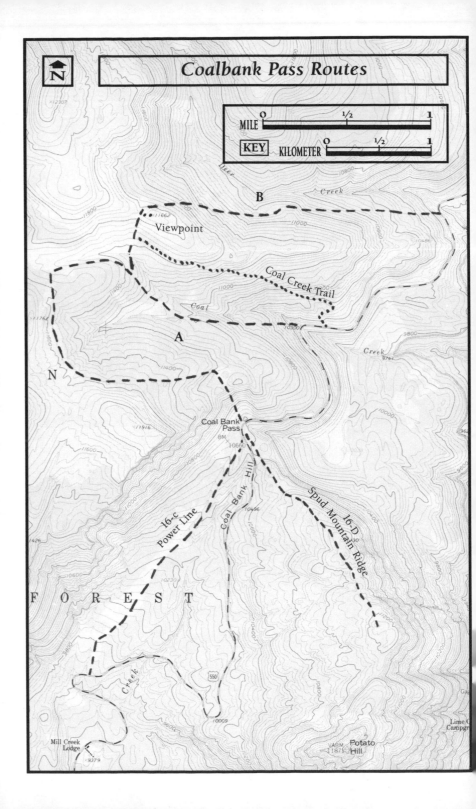

16

Coalbank Pass Routes

Starting elevation: 10,640 feet (3243 meters)
Map: 7.5' Engineer Mountain

From the intersection of 32nd Street and Main Avenue in Durango, it is 32 miles north on U.S. Highway 550 to the summit of Coalbank Pass (8.6 miles north of Purgatory Ski Area). There is room for several cars to park on the east side of the summit.

All ski routes from here are for skiers of intermediate to advanced ability; there is nothing on this pass for beginner or novice skiers. The terrain in all directions is steep, rough, and forested.

A

C O A L   C R E E K

Distance: 5 miles (8 kilometers) one way
Elevation change: Up 1000 feet (305 meters),
    down 1360 feet (415 meters)
High point: 11,660 feet (3554 meters)
Rating: Advanced
Time allowed: 4 hours
Avalanche danger: High

This route, used by skiers seeking steep shots in tree powder on the north-facing slope above Coal Creek, should not be skied in times of high avalanche danger. Avalanche safety training and expert ski technique are essential safety measures for skiing this area. The ability to descend in control may be vital to avoiding injury on the very steep, heavily forested slopes which this route descends.

From the western side of the summit of Coalbank Pass, the route starts right off with a steep climb. This section presents a high and unavoidable avalanche hazard. Zig-zag up the strip of sparse trees between the open slopes on the right and the left. Head for the lowest point on the height above, where the grade starts to lessen and eventually levels out on a little plateau with a small lake. This is 520 feet above Coalbank Pass. From here, it helps if you are familiar with the summer hiking trail to Engineer Mountain, which you follow to the west. It stays to the right of a stream which comes down from that direction. Beyond the stream to the left (south), cornices above steep slopes on peak 11,916 create extreme avalanche danger.

The Engineer Mountain Trail leads you up at a moderately steep grade to treeline. Follow the upper edge of the forest around to the right, traversing with a little elevation gain. Treeline leads you around until you are heading north. Stay east of and below an 11,762-foot knoll; you pass through some trees. Continuing north, you come to an open bowl-like area at the head of the northern fork of Coal Creek.

From here, the route turns right and heads down, staying on the right side of the creek to remain on the north-facing slope all the way down. Before starting down, a short side trip for a view is worthwhile; you have certainly earned it with your strenuous climb. Continue up and northeast to the top of the ridge just ahead, then take a right turn staying on the ridgeline. This leads you to the top of an 11,662-foot point with a panoramic view. Backtrack to the top of the open bowl-like area and start down.

The run down to treeline is wide open, providing a good chance to get your turns going. Heading off into the timber to the south of the creek (to stay on the north-facing slope), you alternate traverses away from the creek with downhill shots all the way down. Avoid getting into the creekbed, which can lead you into steep-walled gullies which present high avalanche danger. As you zig-zag down, your route roughly parallels the creek on the south but always stays above it. Just before you reach the highway, a cliff band leaves you only a narrow lane fairly close to the creek to get through. You emerge at a point on Highway 550 which is 1.2 miles north of and 340 feet below the summit of Coalbank Pass.

This point is on a hairpin curve along Highway 550 where Coal

Northern face of Engineer Mountain from treeline on route to Coal Creek.
Tour 16-A

Creek intersects the road. About a hundred yards down the highway from the creek, the Coal Creek hiking trail begins with an ascent of a steep slope. This trail provides an alternate ski route to the bowl at the head of Coal Creek. The trailhead is marked with a small sign which may be snow-covered at times. There is a parking space across the road from the trailhead.

The steep slope at the trailhead gets a great deal of sun and may have poor snow conditions. This section is short, however. Above, the grade of the trail moderates and the forest shades the snow.

The Coal Creek Trail climbs steadily at a moderately steep grade for about 2 miles and emerges from the trees into the open bowl-like area at the head of the northern fork of Coal Creek. From the bowl, there are three options for the descent: to descend the north-facing slope to the south of the gully of Coal Creek as described above; to return down the Coal Creek Trail (since the trail is on a south-facing slope, snow conditions are not likely to be as good as on north-facing slopes); or to climb over the ridge to the west of peak 11,662 and descend the north-facing slope above Deer Creek as described below.

B

D E E R C R E E K

Distance: 6 miles (9.6 kilometers) one way
Elevation change: Up 970 feet (296 meters),
    down 1800 feet (549 meters)
High point: 11,610 feet (3539 meters)
Rating: Advanced
Time allowed: 5 hours
Avalanche danger: High

Deer Creek is the next stream north from Coal Creek, and the north-facing slope above it provides similar skiing. To reach Deer Creek, follow the directions for the Coal Creek tour to the open bowl-like area at the head of the northern fork of Coal Creek. Either of the two approaches — from the top of Coalbank Pass, or up the Coal Creek Trail — can be used. The figures in the heading apply to a tour which takes the route from the top of Coalbank Pass.

From the bowl at the head of Coal Creek, continue north, climbing over the ridge to the west of peak 11,662. On the other side of the ridge, you can start down the southern fork of Deer Creek, staying right of the creek on the north-facing slope. Stay out of the creek gully, which drops in waterfalls over two cliff bands on its way down. As at Coal Creek, you alternate traverses away from the creek with downhill shots. You end up at the hairpin turn on Highway 550 where Deer Creek intersects the road; be alert for a cliff band here which necessitates a short detour for the final drop to the highway. This point on Highway 550 is 1.4 miles north of the hairpin turn at Coal Creek and 2.6 miles north of the top of Coalbank Pass.

Starting down the Power Line Run.
Tour 16-C

C

P O W E R   L I N E   R U N

Distance: 2 miles (3.2 kilometers) one way
Elevation change: Down 1010 feet (308 meters)
Low point: 9650 feet (2941 meters)
Rating: Intermediate
Time allowed: Half an hour
Avalanche danger: Moderate

From Coalbank Pass, this route descends along a swath cleared of trees for a power line. If it is lacking in unspoiled wilderness quality, it more than makes up for it in sheer cross-country downhill fun.

This was once Durango's ski area, in a time well before Purgatory came along. These old-timers skied from Coalbank Pass to the Mill Creek Lodge; now, the lodge is closed, but most of the ski run is still on public land.

Just south of the summit of Coalbank Pass on the western side of the highway, one of the power line poles has a snow depth gauge on it. From here, you can see a fenced enclosure just ahead. Head for it;

the best way to reach it is around to the right with a short climb through the timber. The way down, with the power line blazing the route, is obvious from here.

The descent is not terribly steep in general, though it has a couple of short steep sections. The slope gets some sun; the snow can get crusty during periods with no new precipitation. Fresh powder is not uncommon here, however.

A mile and three-quarters of uninterrupted descent brings you to a spot where an open lane heads off through the trees to the right while the power line continues straight down. The area under the power line becomes brushy a little way below. Here you cross under the power line and find the opening in the trees on your left created by an access road. This road leads you down, crossing under the power line again, and reaches Highway 550 at a point 2.7 miles south of the summit of Coalbank Pass. This is on the first hairpin turn above the Mill Creek Lodge, on the same side of the highway as Engineer Mountain. This spot is just above a rock outcrop with a black, coal-like band in it.

If there is enough parking space plowed out to park a car here clear of the highway, it can serve as your ski lift. However, during much of a typical winter, this is not likely to be the case. You can walk back to the summit of the pass, or cache a bicycle before you ski down for the ride back up. As a cross-country skier, you know you have to work for your downhill runs. You wouldn't, after all, want to become like one of those wimps who ride lifts.

Durango skiers have in the past finished this run by taking the open lane to the right a mile and three-quarters down, which leads to the highway at Mill Creek Lodge. The last few hundred yards that way are private land which is now posted "No Trespassing." The former Mill Creek Lodge is now a private residence and cars cannot be parked there.

D

S P U D   M O U N T A I N   R I D G E

Distance: 4 miles (6.4 kilometers)
Elevation change: 640 feet (195 meters)
High point: 11,280 feet (3438 meters)
Rating: Crazed intermediate
Time allowed: 5 hours
Avalanche danger: Moderate

For a skier who is ready to test his or her endurance against the roughest, meanest sort of backcountry, this is the place to go. Don't be fooled into thinking this route is easy because it involves a little more than 600 feet of climbing. You will swear it was 6000 feet after breaking trail up steep headwalls in deep backcountry snow. You don't have to be an expert skier to do this, but you do have to be strong and more than a little bit crazy.

Simply head southeast from the summit of Coalbank Pass and stay on top of the ridge which leads towards Spud Mountain ("Potato Hill" on USGS maps). As I have warned you, this is easier said than done. The terrain is laid out along the lines of Purgatory Ski Area: steep headwalls alternating with gladed flats. Unlike Purgatory, here you climb the headwalls before descending them.

It is not all struggle, though; the silent forest of subalpine fir and Englemann spruce seems very pristine here.

The distance given in the heading presumes making a 2-mile ascent towards Spud Mountain and then turning back. The top of an 11,280-foot bump on the ridge is the turnaround point; beyond this the ridgeline swings around more to the south and drops down. The very steep slope leading to treeline beyond the sag in the ridge presents high avalanche danger and should be avoided.

On the return, your own tracks will ease your passage across the flats and ample unbroken powder will aid your descent of the steep headwalls. Then it may begin to seem that the skiers who stayed away from the pristine backcountry were the crazy ones.   O

Molas Pass Routes

The 10,900-foot summit of Molas Pass has long been a favorite with Durango and Silverton cross-country skiers. Cleared by a big forest fire over one hundred years ago, the wide-open spaces provide terrain for novice to advanced skiers. A backcountry area, it is a bit rough for those trying cross-country skiing for the first time.

Since it is a backcountry area, Molas never runs out of surprises for more experienced skiers. I have lost count of how many times I have skied here, and I am still finding new slopes and routes on every visit. The three routes listed here are only the tip of the iceberg (perhaps "top layer of the snowpack" would be a better metaphor here) with regards to the many possibilities at Molas. When exploring, bear in mind that it is not far from the highway to some slopes which are steep enough to present avalanche danger. As you climb towards the peaks on either side of the pass, the avalanche danger increases.

A

LITTLE MOLAS LAKE

Distance: 2 miles (3.2 kilometers)
Starting elevation: 10,788 feet (3288 meters)
Elevation change: 117 feet (36 meters)
Rating: Novice
Time allowed: 2 hours
Avalanche danger: Low
Map: 7.5' Snowdon Peak

The alpine grandeur of Molas is not reserved exclusively for expert skiers; novices can share the wide views and high country sunshine on this relatively easy route. The ski route follows the road to Little Molas Lake, which begins on the western side of the highway 0.4 mile north of the summit of Molas Pass. There is usually room for parking here.

Peak 12,849 from Little Molas Lake; the Bear Creek route climbs over the ridge at top left.

The steepest uphill part of this route comes at the start as the road traverses a hillside, bearing left for a short distance. The road generally heads just north of west for the lake, which is about half a mile from the highway in a straight line. The road curves around a bit, however. It stays to the right of the stream which comes down from the lake.

The lake itself, elevation 10,905 feet, is just a flat, white clearing in the sparse forest in winter. Trips up any of the knolls around it will yield interesting mountain views. These same hills provide opportunities for intermediate or better skiers to take short but steep downhill runs.

On sunny winter days, the lake is a pleasant place to linger before returning in your tracks. In fast snow conditions, the descent of the hill back near the highway can be tricky for inexperienced skiers.

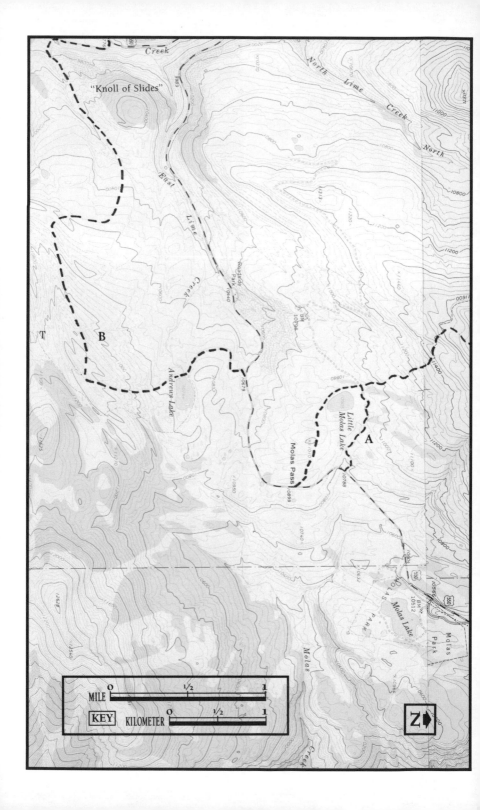

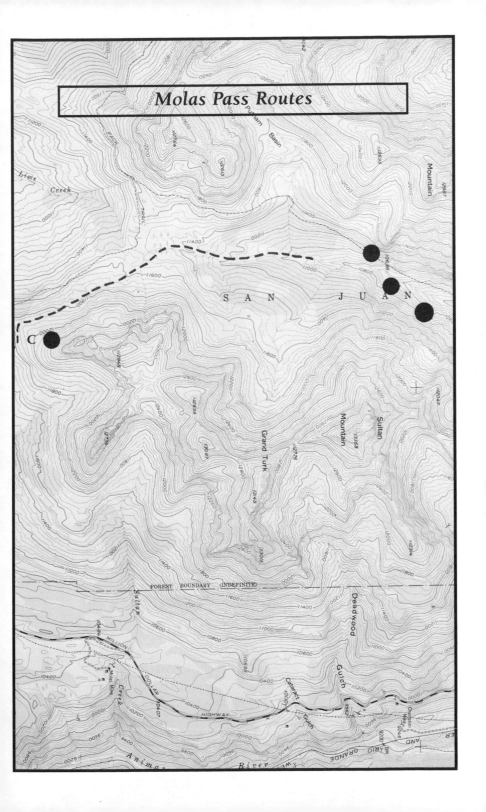

B

A N D R E W S   L A K E   T O   L I M E   C R E E K

Distance: 4 miles (6.4 kilometers) one way
Starting elevation: 10,679 feet (3255 meters)
Elevation change: Up 560 feet (171 meters),
    down 1640 feet (500 meters)
Rating: Intermediate - Advanced
Avalanche danger: Moderate
Map: 7.5' Snowdon Peak

One mile west of the summit of Molas Pass, the Andrews Lake Road heads south from U.S. Highway 550. Parking on the shoulder of the highway is usually possible here. Skiing up the road for 0.6 mile, gaining a little under 100 feet of elevation, brings you to Andrews Lake. From the western end of the lake — where the dam is — the high point of the route is the top of the hill due south of you. It is another 0.6 mile (straight-line distance) and 500 feet of ascent to get there.

From the top of this 11,240-foot hill, the place where you want to end your descent is due west 2 miles straight-line distance. The gullies between bands of rock outcroppings, which are fun to ski partway down, tend to lead you too far south eventually. If you do ski down them, traverse to the north by the time you are in thick trees.

From the hilltop, you can see a 10,480-foot rounded summit which I call the "Knoll of Slides" below you to the west. It is just north of the stream valley which you must descend to avoid a cliff band at the bottom. The avalanche slope on the western side of this knoll is prominent on the right side of the highway as you round Lime Creek ascending Molas Pass; you do not ski near the avalanche slope on this route. There are, however, a few steep slopes along the descent route which present avalanche danger in unstable snowpack conditions. Most of them can be avoided.

The first part of the descent is open; below, a belt of thick tree growth may have you thrashing around for a bit. You come into the clear again at the stream which leads you down to Lime Creek. The right side of the stream is a safer descent than the left side. Steep slopes above the left bank present high avalanche danger but can be avoided by skiing the right bank.

Just before reaching Lime Creek, it is necessary to cross the stream and make the last drop down to the south of it (left as you descend). The last pitch is steep and rough even on the left side; there are cliffs on the right side. At Lime Creek, there is a one-log-wide trail bridge a hundred yards downstream.

The trail will lead you on a short but rough climb up the other bank to the Old Lime Creek Road. Turn right, following the road north one-half mile to the highway. The Andrews Lake Road is then up the highway 3.4 miles to your right. There is usually room to park one or two cars at this end of the Old Lime Creek Road.

C

B E A R   C R E E K

> *Distance:* 9 miles (14.4 kilometers)
> *Starting elevation:* 10,900 feet (3322 meters)
> *Elevation change:* 2020 feet (616 meters)
> *High point:* 11,880 feet (3621 meters)
> *Rating:* Advanced
> *Time allowed:* 6 hours
> *Avalanche danger:* Moderate - High
> *Maps:* 7.5' Snowdon Peak
>   7.5' Silverton
>   San Juan County (topographic)

Strong skiers wanting to get into the backcountry above Molas Pass will find much to both challenge and reward them on a tour into the

Killer avalanche path in the Gulch of Bear Creek
below the turnaround point.
Tour 17-C

gulch of Bear Creek. Head northwest from the summit of the pass, following a ridge to Little Molas Lake. Pass to the west of the lake, losing as little altitude as possible, then start a big climb to the north and west up the open slope ahead. Make for a slope to the left of the 12,849-foot peak above which is the westernmost summit on Grand Turk Mountain. You want to pass to the west of this peak, staying well away from the steep upper slopes just beneath the cliffs on the rocky summit.

The slopes get bigger and steeper as you climb; the steepest slopes here could produce avalanches capable of burying a skier in times of unstable snowpack conditions. It is a 980-foot climb to a high point at 11,880 feet on the shoulder of peak 12,849; this is 2.5 hard miles from the summit of Molas. At this point, treeline is 100 to 200 feet below you on your left; much of the timber is fairly sparse. Continue north, towards the saddle between peak 12,764 of Bear Mountain on the west and peak 12,849. The Bear Creek drainage begins on the other side of this saddle.

After the high point the terrain is moderate, and slopes steep enough to present high avalanche danger can be avoided for the next

2 miles. The fairly short section of skiing above treeline, with its wide views, puts the skier on the edge of Heaven. The run down the other side of the saddle may get you thinking of an angel's flight, gliding down open slopes at a grade suitable for intermediate telemarkers. Enjoy it while it lasts; Hell lies below.

The values given in the heading apply to a tour which descends the canyon of Bear Creek for about a mile and then turns back. Turn around before reaching the area where there is a very steep slope which comes down from cliffs directly above the creek on the left. The canyon of Bear Creek below the turnaround point becomes a Hell's kitchen of avalanche danger where monstrous slidepaths from both sides meet on the bottom. The slidepaths cannot be avoided.

Skiers have descended this way, ending up near the Columbine Restaurant just west of Silverton. Such a tour can only be attempted safely by parties with extensive avalanche safety experience and equipment in times of low avalanche danger.

At the turnaround point a mile down Bear Creek, the elevation is about 10,840 feet. The climb back up to the high point is 1040 feet. From the high point, you have 980 feet of descent back to Molas Pass. This last descent has more steepness than the run down Bear Creek; skiers who have skied Purgatory will find the headwall-and-bench layout of the terrain familiar.

O

Dolores to Telluride

Forest roads in the Dolores District of the San Juan National Forest provide a wealth of cross-country skiing opportunities, some of them in areas where winter use has traditionally been very light. The telephone number for the Dolores Ranger District Office is 303 882-7296. At Lizard Head Pass, which forms the boundary with the Uncompahgre National Forest, skiers of all levels of ability can enjoy a snow season which lasts from November into April. The portion of the Uncompahgre National Forest near Telluride is served by the Norwood District Office, telephone 303 327-4261. The historic mining town of Ophir and the groomed trails of the Telluride Nordic Center add to the variety of skiing available in this region.

Mileages from Dolores used in the driving directions which follow are measured from the city park at the northern end of town. Mileages from Telluride include the 3 miles of spur road C145 which link the town with the main part of Colorado Highway 145.

O

18

Dunton

Distance: 5-10 miles (8-16 kilometers)
Starting elevation: 8850 feet (2697 meters)
Elevation change: 940-1150 feet (287-351 meters)
High point: 9790-10,000 feet (2984-3048 meters)
Rating: Novice - Intermediate
Time allowed: 4-7 hours
Avalanche danger: Low
Map: 7.5' Dolores Peak

From Dolores, it is 12.25 miles east (from Telluride, 51 miles south and west) on Colorado Highway 145 to the West Dolores Road, which heads north beside the West Dolores River. Dunton is 22 slow miles in from the highway. The West Dolores Road may be muddy or snow-packed in winter; at such times, four-wheel drive is recommended. Park where the snowplowing stops just across from Dunton and start skiing up the unplowed road ahead.

The rustic group of cabins and the restaurant at Dunton are a resort centered around the Dunton Hot Spring. Guests staying at the cabins ($30 per night for two) can use the springs, which are also available to non-guests for a $5 per person fee. For information, call Outpost Video in Dolores at 303 882-7443. Small indoor and outdoor pools of the rust-colored hot spring water make for pleasant bathing in a backwoods setting.

Skiing up the road from Dunton, you come to a fork in half a mile. Either direction makes a good ski tour. The lesser values for distance, time, and elevation gain given in the heading apply to a tour which takes the left fork at this point; the greater values apply to a longer tour up the right fork.

Taking the left fork, the road climbs steadily through attractive aspen forest for a mile. The route then crosses open meadows with good views of the Dolores Peaks. Two miles from the fork, the intersection with the Groundhog Stock Driveway is reached. A sign here may be buried in the snow, but you will quite likely see fence posts

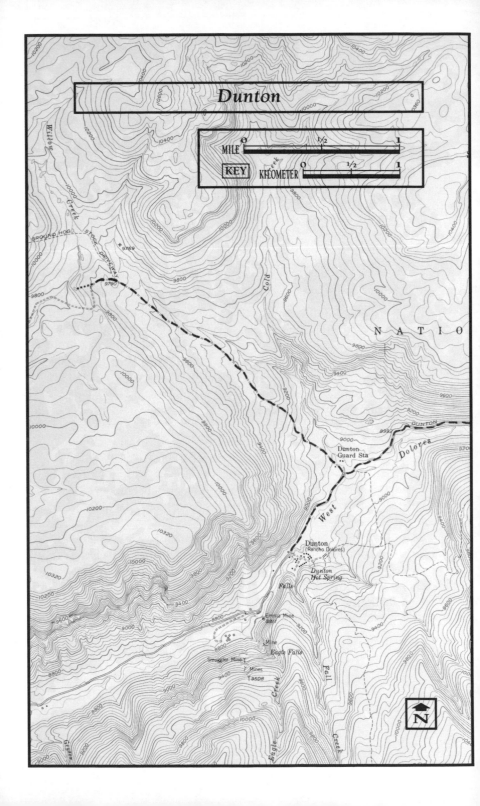

Skiers on the left fork route beneath the Dolores Peaks.

or some other clue that you have reached it.

A little beyond the Groundhog Stock Driveway junction, there are some open slopes steep enough for a little telemarking or other backcountry play. This is the turnaround point for the tour up this fork (the road goes on 17 more miles to the Groundhog Reservoir). Novice skiers can handle this tour in soft snow; if snow conditions are fast, the descent on the return is more of an intermediate run.

Going to the right from the fork half a mile from Dunton, the road leads you by the Burro Bridge Campground in a mile and a half. Burro Bridge itself is crossed half a mile further on; at this point you have gained 300 feet in elevation from Dunton. More serious ascent lies ahead, making intermediate skiing ability necessary for this tour.

In another 0.7 mile you pass the point where the Navajo Lake Trail heads north from the road, which then climbs in earnest for a little over a mile and a half. At last you top out in open meadows, with good views of the Wilson Peaks, 5 miles from Dunton. The elevation here is 10,000 feet; this is the turnaround point for the longer tour described in the heading. If you have time, you can explore the meadows further. They go on for a couple of miles more with little elevation change.

O

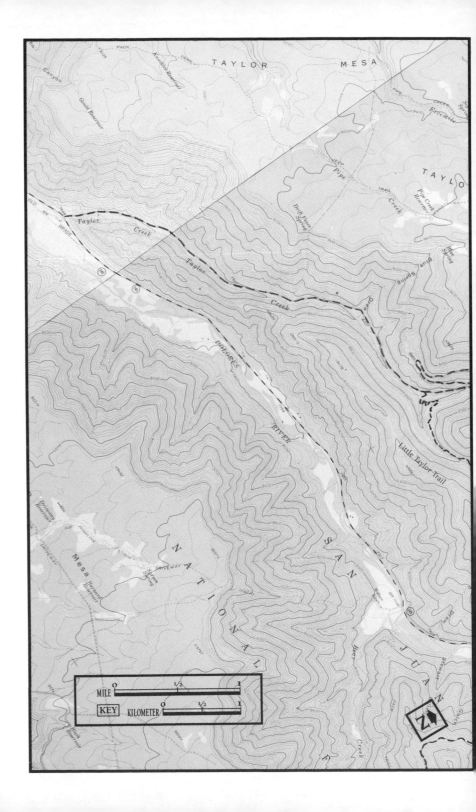

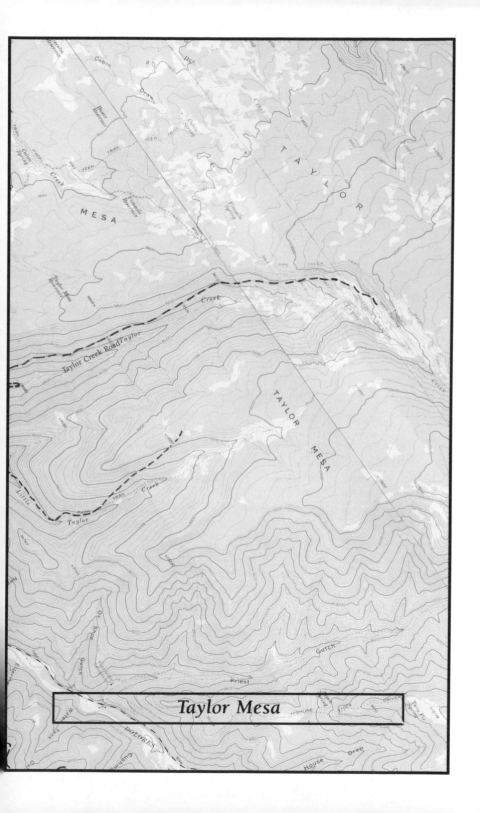

Taylor Mesa

19

Taylor Mesa

Distance: 7-16 miles (11-26 kilometers)
Starting elevation: 7688 feet (2343 meters)
Elevation change: 830-2362 feet (253-720 meters)
High point: 8520-10,050 feet (2597-3063 meters)
Rating: Novice - Intermediate
Time allowed: 4-9 hours
Avalanche danger: Low
Maps: 7.5' Stoner
7.5' Wallace Ranch
7.5' Clyde Lake
San Juan National Forest 1985 Travel Map

The 10,000-foot top of Taylor Mesa is covered with a beautiful coniferous forest which has been logged in some areas and is a forest primeval in others. To reach the top of the Taylor Creek Road and explore its backcountry is a long, ambitious ski tour for a day trip. Winter backpackers could do it in a more leisurely fashion. Novice skiers, however, can enjoy a shorter tour up the first 3 miles of the Taylor Creek Road, and intermediate skiers ready to deal with rough backcountry can explore a shorter but more difficult route using the Little Taylor Trail.

The Taylor Creek Road leaves the northern side of Colorado Highway 145 at a point 18.5 miles east of Dolores (45 miles south and west of Telluride). There may be times during the winter when it is possible, especially with four-wheel drive, to drive in some distance from the highway. This will aid those who want to ski all the way to the mesa top. However, I will describe the route assuming you start skiing at the first cattle guard, which is just off the highway.

The first 3.5 miles of road ascend very gradually on the southern bank of Taylor Creek. A mixed forest of ponderosa pine, aspen, cottonwood, blue spruce, and Douglas fir surrounds you. This section, to the Little Taylor trailhead and back, makes a good 7-mile round trip which novice skiers can handle. The lesser values for distance, elevation gain,

and time allowed in the heading refer to this tour. The snow on this lower-elevation part of the road is most likely to be good from mid-December to March.

The Little Taylor Trail goes off to the right 0.25 mile beyond the third cattle guard, 3.5 miles from the highway. This is a rough and at times obscure route recommended only for intermediate or better skiers. It crosses Taylor Creek and just barely enters the canyon of Little Taylor Creek which comes in from the east at this point. The trail then takes a left to climb steeply up the northern bank of Little Taylor. There is a steep traverse up through evergreens, then a turn at the top which leads to the edge of a clearing. From here you head upstream parallel to Little Taylor Creek, but avoid either descending towards the creek (on your right) or climbing the slope to your left. Fallen aspen make part of this section an obstacle course where you may well have to take your skis off to climb over logs.

One mile from the trailhead (it feels longer), the route takes a right and crosses the creek. For about a mile from the creek crossing, trail blazes consisting of double axe slashes on the trees lead you up the left bank of a tributary stream. The blazes end, leaving you in fairly open aspen-fir woods where there is no sign of any previous human presence. If the idea of skiing trackless wilderness appeals to you, this is your kind of tour.

The mesa top can be reached by climbing the slope on your left, traversing up to the north. A long, slow mile of steep climbing will bring you to the boreal forest where spruce and fir replace aspen. The high point in this area is 10,097 feet; this rugged backcountry route gives you a round trip of 6 miles in addition to 7 miles on the road, with an elevation gain of over 1500 feet from the Little Taylor trailhead.

There are old logging roads on and near the mesa top; not shown on maps, they disappear in clearings and meander around to dead ends in the forest. I found it rewarding to simply wander through what seemed like endless, primeval groves of evergreens, and then to turn around and follow my tracks back out. On the descent, the woods are open enough in many places for fun on the downhill run. And then there is the obstacle course of fallen trees — on the return a sign of nearing trail's end — to make the point that you meet the backcountry on its terms, not your own.

From the Little Taylor trailhead, the Taylor Creek Road makes a 400-foot climb in the next 2 miles around a couple of sharp switchbacks. Continuing to ascend more gradually after that, it reaches a junction with Forest Road 547 at a point 7.7 miles from the highway. In another mile, you enter the coniferous forest of the mesa top just before Forest Road 248, a more primitive road, goes off to the right. From here the possibilities for exploration are endless, but simply making it this far and back in a day trip is a marathon in itself.

O

20

Hillside Drive Road

Distance: 9 miles (14.4 kilometers)
Starting elevation: 8068 feet (2460 meters)
Elevation change: 1132 feet (345 meters)
High point: 9200 feet (2804 meters)
Rating: Novice
Time allowed: 5 hours
Avalanche danger: Moderate
Maps: 7.5' Wallace Ranch
San Juan National Forest 1985 Travel Map

The Hillside Drive Road leads you on a ski tour which traverses the southern wall of the Dolores River Canyon, then turns to follow the tributary gulch of Bear Creek. In 4.5 miles of steady ascent, you climb over 1000 feet from the Dolores at moderate grades through a mixed forest of aspen, Douglas fir, and blue spruce.

On the southern side of Colorado Highway 145 at a point 26 miles east of Dolores (37 miles west and south of Telluride), the Hillside Drive Road crosses the river on a bridge. There is usually room for a couple of cars to park between the highway and the bridge.

Just after skiing across the bridge, the road begins its climb and curves to the west. In the first mile, you turn into Burnette Gulch, the first of many tributary drainages you will cross. Some slopes to the left of the road are steep enough to avalanche; I rate the danger level as moderate here because there was debris from a spring snowslide on the road on one occasion when I skied here in April. There should generally be minimal danger here if the Colorado Avalanche Information Center report rates the avalanche danger level as moderate or low below treeline.

As you enter Burnette Gulch, you can see the road climbing out of the other side; it looks steeper from this angle than it really is. Atop that ascent, you get a nice aerial view of the Circle K Ranch down by the river.

In the next mile, you round Cushman Gulch after crossing a more

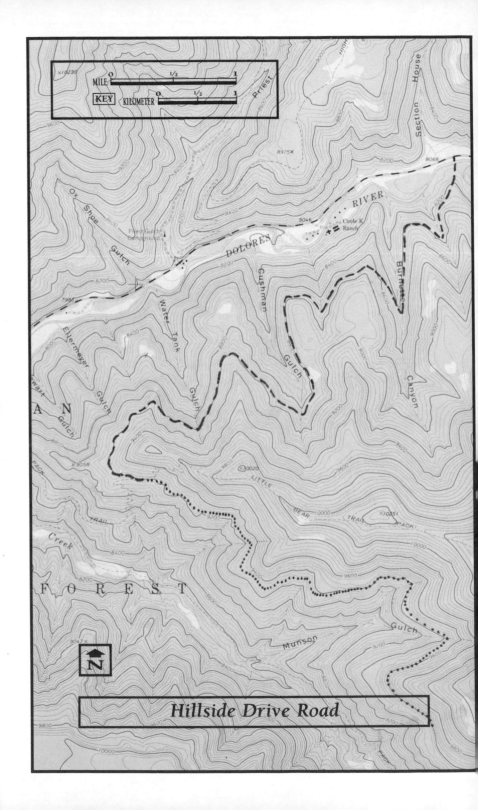

MILE
0   1/2   1

KEY   KILOMETER
0   1/2   1

X10230

8975X

Ox Shoe Gulch

Forest Gulch Campground

DOLORES   RIVER

8046

Circle K Ranch

8068

Section House

HIGH

Cushman Gulch

Buttrette

Canyon

Ehlermeyer Gulch

Water Tank Gulch

wart Gulch

A N

X9058

X10020

LITTLE

BEAR

TRAIL

X10251

PACK

PACK

TRAIL

Creek

F O R E S T

9047X

Munson

Gulch

N

Hillside Drive Road

Ski tracks on Hillside Drive Road.

minor gulch on the way. The road goes on to round Water Tank Gulch. At the top of the climb out of this one, you arrive at a point with a view down to the buildings of Priest Gulch next to the highway. From this point, the road starts a long turn which brings it around to the southeast to enter Bear Creek Canyon. This is the big one, no mere gulch but a canyon miles long.

Just after crossing a cattle guard, you come to a clearing where there is a good view up Bear Creek Canyon. You are high on its northern wall, and can see its course for some distance ahead. Atop the slopes to your south is the relatively flat plateau of Haycamp Mesa, still above you at an elevation of 10,000 feet. Unlike the desert tablelands which come to mind when the term "mesa" is used, the high plateaus in this part of the San Juans support lush evergreen forests.

The road goes on for several miles and can be explored further. The clearing is the turnaround point for the tour described in the heading. The downhill grade should get you back in about half the time the ascent took.

O

21

Scotch Creek

Distance: 6.3 miles (10 kilometers)
Starting elevation: 8600 feet (2621 meters)
Elevation change: 653 feet (199 meters)
High point: 9253 feet (2820 meters)
Rating: Novice
Time allowed: 4 hours
Avalanche danger: Moderate
Maps: 7.5' Rico
              7.5' Hermosa Peak

From Dolores, it is 33 miles east on Colorado Highway 145 to the point where the Scotch Creek Road heads off to the right from the highway just beyond the creek. This spot is on the left 2.5 miles south of Rico and 30 miles west and south of Telluride. The only place to park is on the shoulder of the highway, which may not be clear of snow during and just after storms. At such times you would have to shovel out a parking space to keep the shoulder clear for snow removal; most skiers will probably want to wait until after the plows have done their work. The canyon of Scotch Creek holds plenty of snow. There is no reason to rush out and ski it in the middle of a blizzard.

An interpretive sign at the trailhead gives you a bit of the history of the Pinkerton Trail and Scotch Creek Toll Road which opened up this route a hundred years ago. The road now provides easy skiing in an attractive canyon. Staying on the left bank of the creek, the road meanders with the stream along the canyon bottom. The canyon walls are steep and high most of the way. There could be some avalanche danger from steep, open slopes to the left of the road at times when the danger level for avalanches below treeline is rated high.

Half a mile in, you pass between cliff walls which give you the feeling of passing through a stony gateway into the kingdom of the mountain gods. At a couple of points farther on, the canyon widens. About 2 miles in, a clearing on the left looks like a route uphill; stay

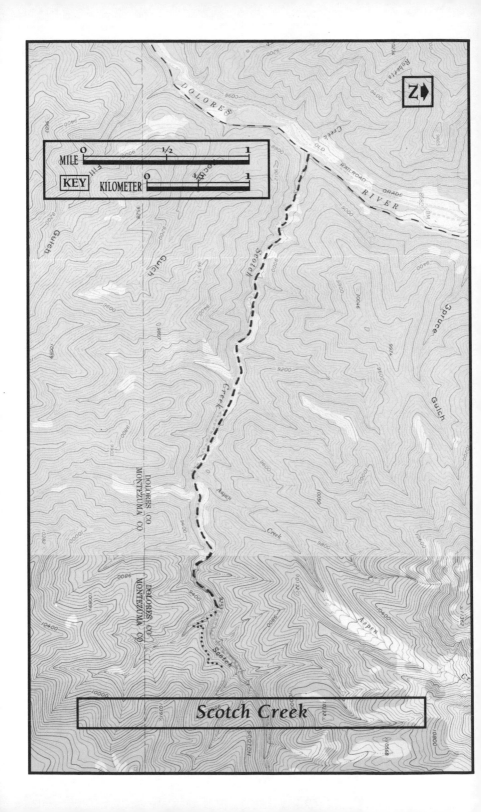

Scotch Creek

Skiing past the cliffs in the canyon of Scotch Creek.

right and on the flat with the creek.

A little over 3 miles in, the road crosses the creek over a culvert and heads uphill on the right bank. This is the turnaround point for the tour described in the heading.

○

22

Lizard Head Pass Routes

The 10,250-foot summit of Lizard Head Pass is a little over 15 miles west and south of Telluride on Colorado Highway 145 (48 miles east and north of Dolores). As the watershed between the San Miguel and Dolores Rivers, it forms the boundary between San Miguel and Dolores counties. At this elevation, the snow is typically good for skiing from November into April.

A
T   H   E   M   E   A   D   O   W

Distance: 4 miles (6.4 kilometers)
Starting elevation: 10,240 feet (3121 meters)
Elevation change: 200 feet (61 meters) down
   and back up
Rating: Beginner - Novice
Time allowed: 3 hours
Avalanche danger: Low
Map: 7.5' Mount Wilson

The open meadow which parallels the highway on the southeastern side is a good place for beginner skiers to get a small taste of the boreal forest backcountry. From the summit of the pass, where parking space is available, ski southwest down the meadow across the highway from the Lizard Head Pass sign. Along the way, skiing further from the road will take you into the trees. Exploring open lanes in the forest here is an introduction to wilderness skiing in an area where slopes are gentle. Some spots may be rough for first-time skiers, but you are never far from the meadow where the going is easy.

The basic route for this tour consists of going 2 miles down the meadow. At this point, there is a view of the distinctive shaft of Lizard Head Peak in the distance across the highway. Below this, the terrain

Dolores to Telluride

gets steeper; you can see the highway start to descend more rapidly and become more walled-in ahead. Turn back and ski uphill to the point where you started.

B

C R O S S   M O U N T A I N   T R A I L

> **Distance:** 4-7 miles (6.4-11.2 kilometers)
> **Starting elevation:** 10,080 feet (3072 meters)
> **Elevation change:** 1200-1840 feet (366-561 meters)
> **High point:** 11,280-11,920 feet (3437-3633 meters)
> **Rating:** Intermediate - Advanced
> **Time allowed:** 3-6 hours
> **Avalanche danger:** Low - High
> **Map:** 7.5' Mount Wilson

A tour 2 miles up this trail for skiing in the trees is relatively free from avalanche danger. Continuing to the alpine tundra of the Lizard Head Wilderness Area exposes the skier to areas of high avalanche danger, much of which can be avoided by intelligent route-finding. Topographic map and compass are essential on this route.

The trailhead for the Cross Mountain Trail is located 2 miles southwest of the summit of Lizard head Pass on the northwestern side of the highway. At this point there is a view of the shaft of Lizard Head Peak to the north. There may be parking room plowed out at this point, but this is not always the case. At worst, it is always possible to park at the top of the pass and ski two miles down the meadow to reach this trailhead.

The trail can be hard to follow for the first half mile because it passes through some clearings where its route is obscure. In the trees, the trail is usually a distinct open lane of jeep road width. It starts at a trailhead sign which is about 200 yards northwest (compass bearing

129

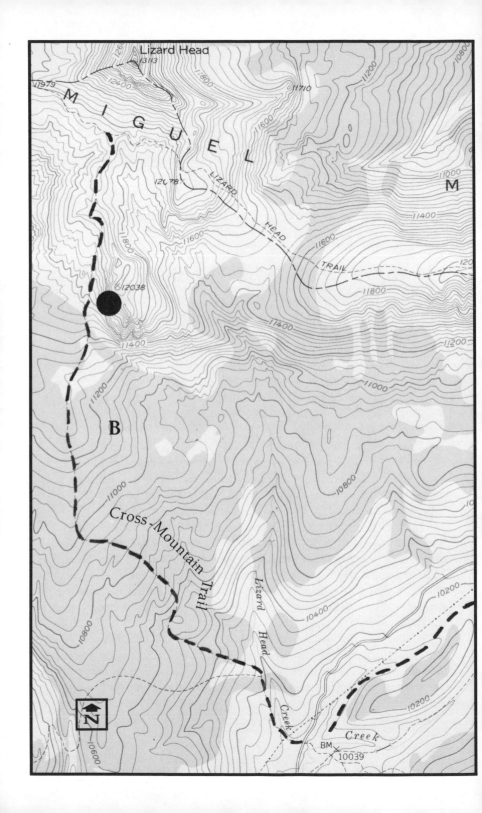

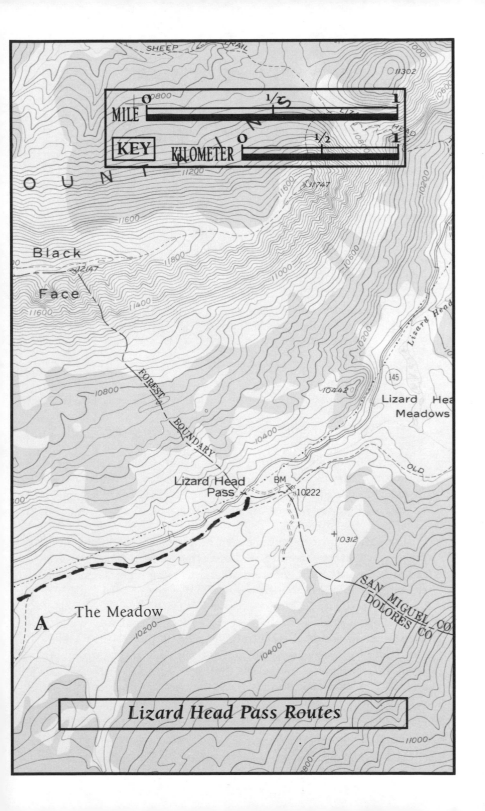

SHEEP TRAIL

○ 11302

KEY

MILE 0   1/2   1

KILOMETER 0   1/2   1

MOUNTIONS

11747

Black

Face
12147

FOREST BOUNDARY

145

10448

Lizard Head
Meadows

Lizard Head Pass

BM 10222

OLD

+ 10312

SAN MIGUEL CO
DOLORES CO

A   The Meadow

Lizard Head Pass Routes

Steve Bortz telemarking on the tundra beneath Lizard Head Peak.
Tour 22-B

300 degrees) from the highway at the clearing with a view of Lizard Head Peak. The trailhead is to the left of the gully of Lizard Head Creek.

From the sign, the trail starts climbing, always staying left of the creek and not descending at all. Take a compass bearing on Lizard Head Peak before the trees hide it; this should be about 315 degrees northwest, and will be a useful point for keeping oriented if you should lose the trail. It could be easy if other skiers have left tracks for you — if they knew where they were going. You cannot count on either being the case.

For about a quarter mile the trail heads straight for Lizard Head Peak, then it swings more to the west. This is the point where it is easiest to lose it. Some scouting around to locate the trail where it enters the timber may well be necessary. After the first half mile, the trail stays mostly in dense forest where it is easier to follow.

The uphill grade is fairly steep at times and continues without letup. Somewhat under 2 miles from the trailhead you cross the wilderness boundary; the sign will probably be buried in the snowpack. At about the 2-mile point, you enter a clearing where you see Lizard Head again after a long time during which the trees have hidden it from

view. This clearing is the turnaround point for the shorter tour outlined in the heading. If the avalanche danger above treeline is rated high, all skiers should turn back from this point.

Treeline is half a mile ahead through a last belt of forest. Just after emerging from the trees, the trail traverses a very steep slope which presents very high avalanche danger. Alternate routes should be considered. The ascent of the tundra heads north towards Lizard Head; stop at a safe distance from the steep slopes on the southern face of the peak. This point is a hard 3.2 miles from the trailhead; with the climbing, it feels longer.

If the snow conditions are at all reasonable, the return trip should take no more than one-quarter the time of the ascent. This is a route for skiers confident of their downhill control. The long run back down through the trees is a memorable one, especially if a few inches of fresh powder have fallen in the boreal forest.

O

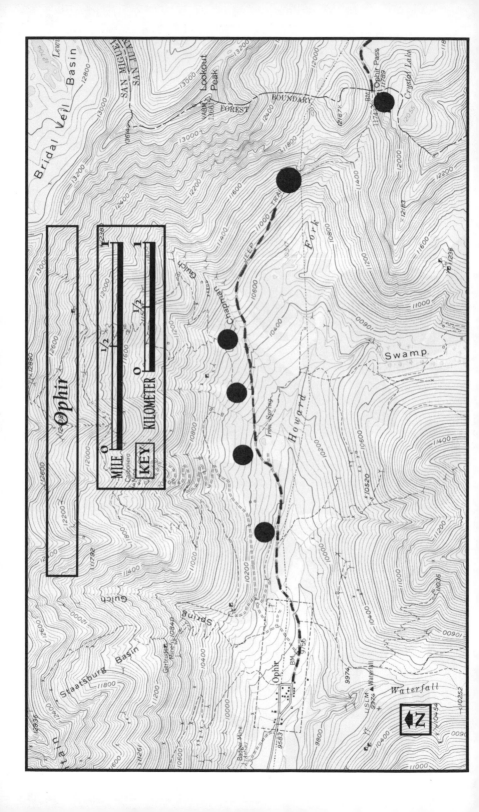

23

Ophir

Distance: 5 miles (8 kilometers)
Starting elevation: 9756 feet (2974 meters)
Elevation change: 1244 feet (379 meters)
High point: 11,000 feet (3353 meters)
Rating: Intermediate
Time allowed: 4 hours
Avalanche danger: Moderate - High
Map: 7.5' Ophir

The side road to Ophir from Colorado Highway 145 is marked by the unmistakable rock pinnacles of the Ophir Needles, 10.5 miles from Telluride and 53 miles from Dolores. It is 2 miles west on the side road to the town. Take the right-hand street as you enter the settled area and find a parking space. Space could be tight here at times when the snowbanks are piled high; be considerate of the residents.

On the drive into Ophir you see many huge slidepaths. Take note of the status of the ones to the left; thay have about the same slope and aspect as some which cross the ski route ahead.

The ski route follows the jeep road towards Ophir Pass. This road continues straight ahead from the end of the right-hand (southern-most) street in town. For the first half mile, skiing is flat and in the open. Just after crossing under a power line, the road enters the trees.

In less than a mile, you reach a point where a side road heads right and downhill and a washout crosses the main road. Just beyond is the first of four big slidepaths that come down from the left and cross the road. You ski across the runout zones of these slidepaths on moderate slopes where your skiing is unlikely to trigger an avalanche. However, there is danger here in times when natural releases above are likely; this route should definitely not be skied in times of high avalanche danger. You are skiing well below treeline here, but the slidepaths have their starting zones above treeline.

Novice skiers can take a short tour on this route by going only as far as the edge of the second slidepath. This is a round trip of a bit over 2 miles.

Beyond the first slidepath, the road begins to climb more steeply. A little over a mile from the trailhead, you cross the second slidepath. It is another quarter mile to the third one and about one-third mile further to the fourth. This fourth slidepath, which comes down Chapman Gulch, is about the size of an Alaskan glacier. If there is rough and icy avalanche debris at this point, you may want to turn around from here. Beyond, the views are interesting and you gain some additional altitude for a downhill run on the return, but crossing avalanche crud at a moderately steep grade can be nothing but a hassle.

Beyond the fourth slidepath, a half-mile climb through the last belt of trees takes you to treeline at about 11,000 feet. The skiing on this stretch of road in the forest can be good. Treeline is the turnaround point here; the jeep road ahead traverses an extremely steep slope where you would be skiing in the middle of a killer avalanche zone for a long time. The probability of skier-triggered avalanches there is high.

The view from treeline encompasses mountain terrain so rugged as to be frightening. Ophir Pass lies at the head of the gulch above, its true summit hidden around a bend. It can be reached on skis by strong intermediate and advanced skiers from the other side, near Silverton; see Tour 28 "Ophir Pass: Eastern Side" on page 159.

O

24

Telluride Nordic Center

Post Office Box 307
Telluride, Colorado 81435
303 728-3404

Maintained tracks for all ability levels
Distance: 9.5 miles (15 kilometers)
Starting elevation: 9600 feet (2926 meters)
Trail fee: $4 adult; $2 child under 12
Equipment rental: $8/day; $6/half day (noon)
Trail map: Available at touring center

From the spur road C145 turnoff 3 miles west of the town of Telluride, it is 1.25 miles south on Colorado Highway 145 to the ski area access road which leads to the Meadows Base Facility. After taking a left onto the access road, you will reach the Nordic Center in half a mile.

Trails at the Telluride Nordic Center meander through aspen groves and open meadows which have the most vertical relief of any touring center in southwestern Colorado. The center also offers a full program of instruction, racing, and guided backcountry tours. Clinics (group lessons) in general Nordic technique, skating, and telemarking are given on a regularly scheduled basis; call or write for current information on times and rates. Touring and skating equipment is available at the Nordic Center. Telemarking equipment can be rented from ski shops in town.

Guided backcountry tours include a trip which rides up on the lifts, then tours through Prospect Basin, an area which might someday be developed as an addition to the alpine slopes. This is for intermediate to advanced skiers; other trips suitable for skiers of all levels of ability are also available.

○

*Bill Dunkelberger
conducts a skating
clinic.*

Additional Areas
Dolores to Telluride

S T O N E R   L O D G E

25134 Highway 145
Dolores, Colorado 81323
303 882-7825

The former downhill ski area at Stoner no longer operates. However, telemarkers willing to climb the 1200-foot slopes under their own power may ski the area. Really ambitious tourers could go on to ski on top of Haycamp Mesa after climbing the ski slope.

The Stoner Lodge is open all winter, with reasonably priced accommodations and full restaurant and bar service. Situated south of Colorado Highway 145 at a point 14 miles from Dolores and 49 miles from Telluride, it is conveniently located for access to cross-country skiing routes in this area.

R O A R I N G   F O R K S   R O A D

This forest road is located a little over 27 miles east of Dolores (36 miles west and south of Telluride) on the southern side of Colorado Highway 145. It provides skiing very similar to the Hillside Drive Road (see tour description above, Tour 20), except that it leaves the Dolores River quickly to follow the tributary canyon of Roaring Forks Creek.

O

139

Ouray-Ridgway Area

Ski routes in this area are primarily in the Ouray District of the Uncompahgre National Forest, telephone 303 249-3711. Red Mountain Pass is the boundary with the San Juan National Forest. The Uncompahgre National Forest Map is the best for an overview of the area. For backcountry information, Big Horn Mercantile at 309 Main Street in Ouray, telephone 303 325-4257, is a good place to check; they can put you in touch with local guide services.

One of the principal apres-ski attractions of Ouray is the municipal hot springs pool, telephone 303 325-4638, which is open to the public for a charge of $3.75 per person. Ten miles north of Ouray, Colorado Highway 62 heads west from Ridgway, giving access to some nearby ski touring areas and continuing 41 miles to Telluride.

O

25

The Amphitheater

Distance: 1.5-3.7 miles (2.4-6 kilometers)
Starting elevation: 8120 feet (2475 meters)
Elevation change: 340-1200 feet (104-366 meters)
High points: 8460-9320 feet (2579-2841 meters)
Rating: Intermediate - Advanced
Time allowed: 2-5 hours
Avalanche danger: Low - Moderate
Maps: 7.5' Ouray
    Ouray County Cross-Country Skiing Guide

One mile south of Ouray on U.S. Highway 550, after the second switchback, the road to the Amphitheater Campground heads off to the left. In winter, a gate 0.1 mile from the highway is closed (at the bridge over Portland Creek). A hundred feet before the gate, the un-plowed Portland Mine Road heads uphill to the right; beyond the gate, the Amphitheater Campground Road continues. These two roads give access to a trail network which provides a variety of possibilities for ski touring.

The Amphitheater Campground Road ascends 340 feet in 0.75 mile to a trailhead sign where the road ends. A trip this far and back makes a pleasant short tour with fine views over Ouray. Good novice skiers can handle the road grade back down in soft snow. Fast snow conditions are more common on this stretch of road, however, making it an intermediate run most of the time. The lesser values for distance, elevation gain, and time given in the heading apply to this tour.

The campground loop road branches off to the right a little before the end of the road; it is steeper, curvier, and narrower than the access road. An attractive evergreen forest grows in the campground area, making a side trip through the campground loops an enjoyable one. Doing all the loops adds somewhat over half a mile to the tour up and down the access road.

More difficult backcountry routes go on from the trailhead at the end of the access road. Be prepared for map and compass work. The

141

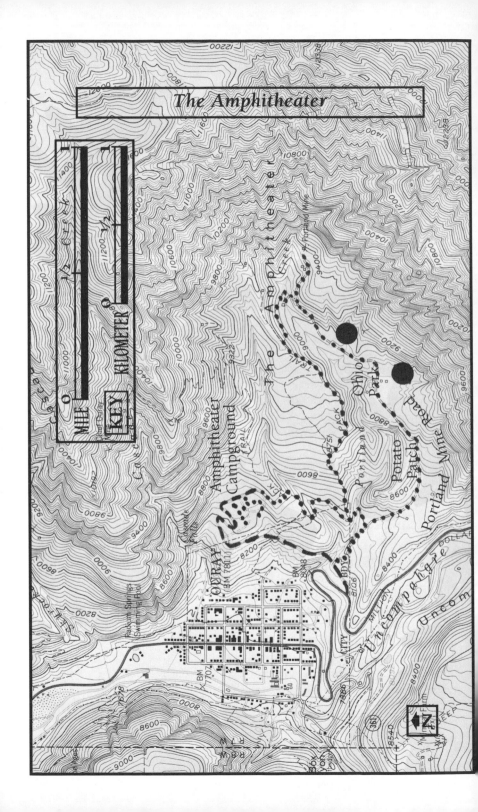

trail heads to the right from the end of the road, traversing a slope above the campsites, then climbs to a ridge where a branch trail heads uphill to the left. This first branch trail, about one-quarter mile from the trailhead, is not good for skiing; continue on the main trail. It descends 300 feet in the next third of a mile to a stream crossing.

On the way, you need to make a left turn at a trail junction in the woods which may be obscure in the snow if there are no ski tracks to follow. At the junction, which is in a small open area, the trail turns from heading southwest to heading just east of south for a short time, then just north of east as it descends to the stream crossing. On the other side of the stream, climbing out at a steep grade, the trail curves around to the right, heading south and then southwest again.

About a third of a mile from the stream crossing, another branch trail heads up a ridge to the left. This one can be skied by advanced skiers; it climbs 720 feet in a mile to reach the Portland Mine Road, which provides a route back down. The greater values for distance, time, and elevation gain given in the heading apply to this quite difficult loop tour. The path of the Portland Slide crosses the Portland Mine Road about half a mile down from the Portland Mine. This route should not be skied in times of high avalanche danger.

Continuing on the main trail from the point where the Portland Mine route branches off, the trail swings left (to the east) and descends to Portland Creek, which it crosses on a bridge. The route then follows an old road out to the Portland Mine Road. Turning right here brings you back to your car in one-quarter mile of descent. The total distance for this loop tour is just over 2 miles with 560 feet of elevation gain.

Other possibilities for touring in this area involve skiing up the Portland Mine Road. A tour to the "Potato Patch," a big open field half a mile up the road on the right, is an intermediate trip. A tour a mile up the road to Ohio Park is for more advanced skiers, who can find short steep slopes in the area. The Ohio Park Slide enters Ohio Park from the south; avoid its runout zone.

O

143

26

East Dallas Creek

Distance: Up to 14 miles (22 kilometers) round trip
Starting elevation: 7758 feet (2365 meters)
Elevation change: Up to 1602 feet (488 meters)
High point: 9360 feet (2853 meters)
Rating: Novice - Intermediate
Avalanche danger: Low
Map: 7.5' Mount Sneffels

From Ridgway, take Colorado Highway 62 west for 4.8 miles and take a left onto the East Dallas Creek Road (Ouray County Road 7). Follow the signs for the Uncompahgre National Forest. Two miles from the highway, park where the plowing stops and ski ahead on the unplowed road.

You are in pinyon and juniper at the start, but the snowmaking power of Mount Sneffels reigns here, and the snow cover is deeper than in most pinyon-juniper areas. The road switchbacks upward not far from where you started skiing. It continues a long but gradual climb most of the time on the way to the national forest boundary 5 miles from where you parked.

The land on either side of the road up to the forest boundary is private property. Public access is limited to the road itself until you cross the national forest boundary.

A tour of any length on this road is worthwhile for the view of the Sneffels Range ahead. The 7-mile trip all the way to the end of the road has its attractions. You reach the boundary of the Mount Sneffels Wilderness Area, where the transition to spruce-fir forest beneath the sheer northern face of Mount Sneffels is abrupt.

O

Linda Faldetta descends the East Dallas Creek Road.

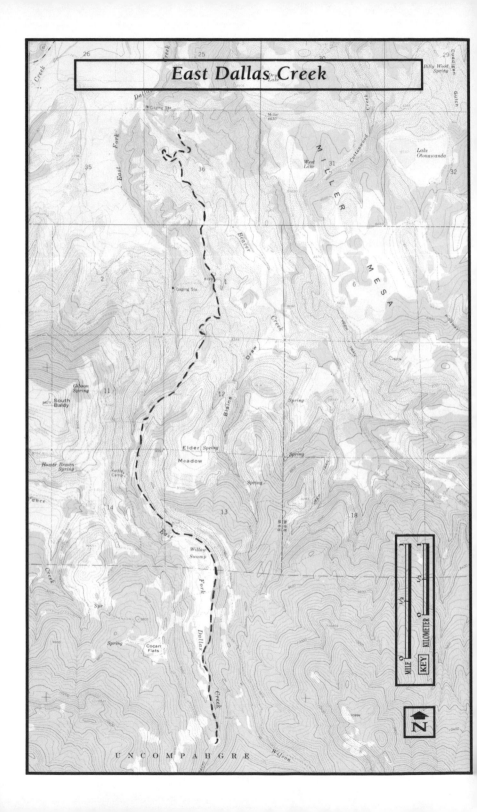

27

Red Mountain Pass Routes

Starting elevation: 11,075 feet (3376 meters)
Map: 7.5' Ironton

Advanced Nordic skiers and backcountry alpine tourers have long been drawn to this pass, where treeline is near at hand in either direction. The terrain is generally not for beginners or novices, with the exception of novice skiers heading for the St. Paul Lodge, whose approach route will be quite challenging for them.

A THE LAKES

Distance: 2 miles (3.2 kilometers)
High point: 11,400 feet (3475 meters)
Rating: Intermediate
Time allowed: 2 hours
Avalanche danger: Moderate
Map: 7.5' Ironton

Intermediate skiers wishing to explore Red Mountain Pass can have fun touring and playing on the slopes just west of the summit of the pass. The half-mile belt of evergreen forest between the highway and treeline has many openings; some of these are small high-altitude lakes. In winter, these are no more than white clearings between the sparse trees.

Zig-zagging up the slopes to treeline is a good piece of work which earns you a wider view. Climbing further gets you into terrain for more advanced skiers and exposes you to a higher avalanche danger. Even the area in the trees should not be skied when the overall avalanche danger level, as reported by the Colorado Avalanche Information

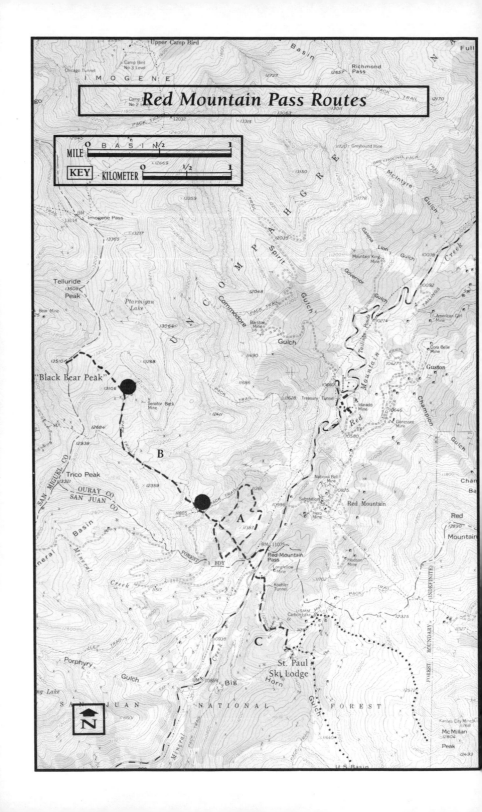

Joan Green and Jim Harvey ready for a spring ascent from the lakes at Red Mountain Pass.

Tour 27-A

Center, is high for Colorado's southern mountains. Avoid skiing in the bottom of steep-walled stream gullies, where enough snow to bury a skier can avalanche off of the sides.

Nothing but the surface of the lakes themselves is flat in this area, so there are ample opportunities for downhill fun. Intermediate skiers become advanced skiers by practicing downhill technique on slopes that can be run again and again. This area is also good for skiers who are not acclimatized to the high altitude; here, though the air is thin, you simply take it easy and allow plenty of time to catch your breath.

B

" B L A C K   B E A R   P E A K "

> *Distance:*   5 miles (8 kilometers) round trip
> *Elevation change:*   2435 feet (742 meters)
> *High point:*   13,510 feet (4118 meters)
> *Rating:*   Advanced
> *Avalanche danger:*   High

This alpine tundra backcountry route takes you to the highest altitude reached by any tour in this book. The 13,510-foot mountaintop which is your destination is unofficially called "Black Bear Peak."

On much of this ski route, the avalanche danger is moderate to low, but two unavoidable steep sections present high danger. Avalanche safety training and equipment are essential for parties skiing this route.

From the summit of Red Mountain Pass, head west (bearing 300 degrees) climbing up through the trees. You reach treeline in half a mile. Just above, the route ascends the first very steep pitch. Stay to the right (north) of a gully which comes down from the direction of Trico Peak. Stay to the left of the rocky cliff bands farther north on the slope ahead.

Topping this tough climb, bear a little more to the north. You are climbing a slope, still moderately steep, between the eastern ridge of Trico Peak to your left and peak 12,411 to your right. There is a little bowl to the right; avoid any descent into it and keep climbing.

The grade moderates within the next mile. A long, mellow ascent brings you to an area where two old cabins stand off to the right. The route heads up a chute here — the second really steep pitch — which is not extreme by alpine standards, but is steep enough to present avalanche danger. Above the chute, the climb is still steep; the peak is somewhat to the left. It is a hard half-mile in the thin air to the summit, at first continuing your northward course, then swinging around more to the west.

The top of the peak is broad. The snow on it is likely to be packed

One of the old cabins at the foot of "Black Bear Peak."
Tour 27-B

hard as cement by the wind; exposed areas may be blown bare. Quite likely you will be exposed to the chilling effect of the prevailing wind from the west. Telluride is visible far below you in that direction. Across Red Mountain Pass to the east, McMillan Peak and U.S. Basin above the St. Paul Lodge are in view. From this viewpoint, they are mere foreground to a San Juan mountain panorama.

This tour is a good one for the spring. Avalanche danger is predictably low early in the morning after a clear night with no new snow. Heat radiates away during a cloudless night, making for a good overnight freeze which stabilizes the snowpack. Corn-snow conditions at mid-morning on a sunny day can be excellent. One factor to keep in mind is the eastern exposure of the slopes used by this ski route.

On the descent from the peak, the top of the chute which you ascended is tricky to find. The cabins below it are not visible from just above. Take care to follow your tracks down so that you find the correct spot. The long mellow section, once below the chute, is easier skiing, even getting too flat at one point on the way down.

The top of the first steep pitch is also tricky to locate on the descent. Remember the little bowl you saw on the way up; the descending route tends to lead you into it. If you do descend to its bottom, you will have to climb up out of it to the right. You may prefer

to contour around, staying high on the right side of the little bowl, where the tracks you made going up should lead you back to the top of that first steep slope. The steep pitch itself is advanced skiing in avalanche terrain.

On the descent from the long, mellow section, avoid going too far to the left. You will wind up above the cliff bands you saw from treeline on the climb up, but you will not be able to see them from above on your way down.

Reaching the summit of a peak this high on skis is a memorable experience. That makes it well worth waiting for the right time, a day with low avalanche danger and good weather. I had to turn back on my first attempt to ski this route because of whiteout conditions in early May; this route cannot be skied safely when visibility is poor.

C
S T . P A U L   S K I   L O D G E

Post Office Box 463
Silverton, Colorado 81302
303 387-5494

Backcountry lodge with tours guided by
    avalanche expert
Distance: 3-4 miles (5-7 kilometers) from lodge
Elevation change: 960-1400 feet (293-427 meters)
    from lodge
High points: 12,360-12,804 feet
    (3767-3903 meters)
Rating: Novice - Advanced; instruction provided
Time allowed: Overnight stay
Avalanche danger: Moderate - High
Map: 7.5' Ironton

The St. Paul Lodge.
Tour 27-C

Just south of the summit of Red Mountain Pass on the eastern side, a jeep road winds its way up a little valley and through the forest to the rustic St. Paul Lodge. The ascent is a steep mile uphill; the lodge sits just below treeline at 11,400 feet. From the lodge, avalanche observer Christopher George — one of the people who provides information to the Colorado Avalanche Information Center in Denver — guides guests on tours to the alpine tundra of U.S. Basin and McMillan Peak.

The rate of $65 per person per night includes lodging, meals, use of a porch full of ski equipment, guide service, instruction, and avalanche safety information. A discount is available for groups of ten or more. Accommodations are primarily bunkrooms; guests bring their own sleeping bags.

The route to U.S. Basin ascends above treeline quickly and continues up the basin to a ridge at 12,360 feet. Advanced skiers can find steep slopes on the wide-open tundra, but many gentler grades provide easier routes. It is about a mile and a half from the lodge to the top of the basin, a tough workout because of the climbing and the thin air.

The route to McMillan Peak (summit 12,804 feet) is a bit longer and climbs more. It is for intermediate to advanced skiers. In winter,

153

the last stretch of climbing from a ridge to the summit is likely to be on windblown or crusty snow; less windblown snow on the rest of the route can provide better skiing. This route can be excellent for spring skiing all the way to the peak. Winter or spring, many other guided backcountry tours can be arranged using the lodge as a base.

○

Additional Areas
Ouray-Ridgway Area

M   I   L   L   E   R   M   E   S   A

(Beginner - Intermediate)

At Ridgway, travel west 0.9 mile on Colorado Highway 62 from U.S. Highway 550 to Ouray County Road 5. This is Amelia Street, which is also designated by the Girl Scout Camp sign. Turn left and head south on County Road 5. In 0.25 mile, turn right at Le Ranch restaurant. Follow this road to Elk Meadows, about 5.5 miles from Highway 62. Park in the plowed area just beyond the entrance to Elk Meadows.

The ski route continues on the unplowed portion of County Road 5, which heads south from the parking area and turns east up the hill. After about a mile, the trail breaks into the open. The most direct route across the meadow to where the trail continues is due south to the top of the ridge. From here the trail is easy to follow downhill to the east. The rest of the route is generally uphill to Coal Creek, about 4.5 miles from where you parked. Public access is limited to the roadway until the Uncompahgre National Forest boundary is crossed at a pipe gate.

O   W   L   C   R   E   E   K   P   A   S   S

(Novice)

Drive north from Ridgway on U.S. Highway 550 for 1.8 miles, then turn right on Ouray County Road 10 at the sign for Owl Creek Pass.

Drive about 6 more miles to the end of the plowed section of the road; park carefully to avoid blocking the road or other cars. Ski along the road towards Owl Creek Pass, which is 7 miles farther; the route is easy for several miles but becomes steeper after entering the aspen forest beyond the national forest boundary.

D E X T E R   C R E E K

(Advanced)

Dexter Creek Road, Ouray County Road 14, leaves U.S. Highway 550 at a 1.8 miles north of the Ouray Hot Springs Pool. Drive past Lake Lenore, bearing right where a road branches off to the left to cross the bridge over Dexter Creek. Plowing ends 1.3 miles from Highway 550; parking space is limited. Ski up the Dexter Creek Road, which crosses and follows the creek; the grade is steep.

A D D I T I O N A L   I N F O R M A T I O N

Ouray County Cross-Country Skiing Guide

The Trail Group, Inc.
Post Office Box 50
Ouray, Colorado 81427

The Trail Group has prepared a pamphlet-sized guide which is available locally or by mail. It contains maps and some additional information on these routes.

○

Silverton and Vicinity

The Town of Silverton is located in Baker's Park, a flat area at an elevation of 9300 feet which is walled in by high peaks. Everywhere you look there are avalanche paths. Snowslides occasionally block U.S. Highway 550 at Red Mountain and Molas passes, sometimes closing highway access to the town for brief periods. Highway crews use heavy artillery to bomb these slidepaths for avalanche control.

Each winter, the Silverton Avalanche School (Post Office Box 4, Silverton, Colorado 81433) offers an intensive three-day workshop to groups which include highway workers, ski patrollers, and recreational skiers. For information you can also contact the Silverton Chamber of Commerce (418 Greene Street, Silverton, Colorado 81433; telephone 303 387-5654).

Though avalanche hazards abound in the terrain around Silverton, the area has much to offer ski tourers with avalanche safety training. The skiing is primarily for strong intermediates and advanced skiers, though there are a couple of routes where novices can go several miles. There are times when the snowpack is "bombproof," so stable that even explosives will not trigger slides; at such times, Silverton is the trailhead for some exciting backcountry skiing.

O

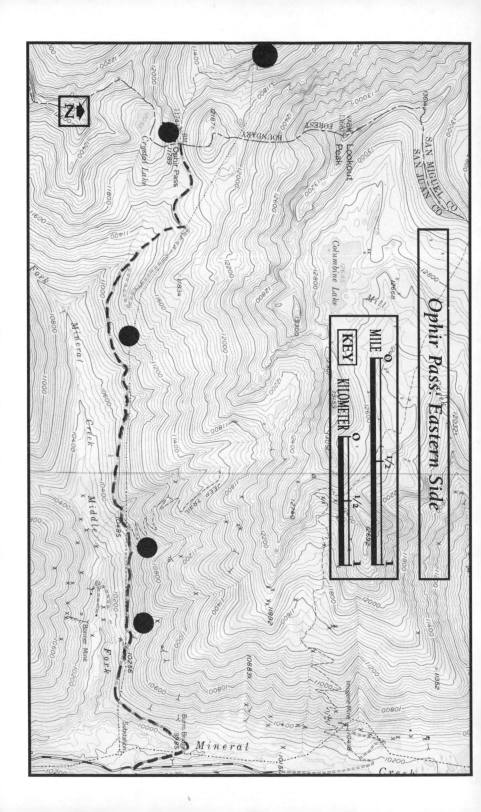

28

Ophir Pass: Eastern Side

Distance: 8.8 miles (14 kilometers)
Starting elevation: 10,085 feet (3074 meters)
Elevation change: 1704 feet (519 meters)
High point: 11,789 feet (3593 meters)
Rating: Intermediate - Advanced
Time allowed: 6-7 hours
Avalanche danger: Moderate - High
Maps: 7.5' Silverton
7.5' Ophir

The Ophir Pass Road is on the western side of U.S. Highway 550 at a point 4.6 miles northwest of Silverton (this is 5 miles south of the summit of Red Mountain Pass). The start of the road is buried in the snowbank at the side of the highway, but a good parking space may be found just east of it, at an access road to an electrical substation.

The Ophir Pass Road descends briefly to the north at the start to cross a bridge over Mineral Creek. Turning to the south, the road traverses up through the aspen and gradually comes around to the west. It traverses the northern wall of the gulch of the Middle Fork of Mineral Creek up to the pass.

In the first 2 miles, the road crosses two major slidepaths. These are obvious open swaths through the trees which may well be covered with rough avalanche debris. The exposure to avalanche danger on them is fairly brief, and it is not likely that a skier-triggered slide would start at the points where you cross them. However, this route should not be skied in times when avalanche danger is high and natural releases above are likely.

After about 2 miles of skiing, you come into the open. From this point on, avalanche danger exists from steep slopes on your right. From here to the pass, always watch the terrain above you.

The snow-buried road becomes obscure. A power line which has followed the road with you goes up the steep slope on the right here; do not follow it. Stay to the left of and below it, traversing up. Stay

above the creek gully on your left.

About a mile from where you came into the open, the creek gully curves around to the northwest as if to "head you off at the pass." The road, probably invisible here, switchbacks up in this area. Bear right and work your way up, heading northwest yourself to keep above the creek. Climb until you rejoin the power line; from here the summit of Ophir Pass is due west.

The power line heads northwest to a saddle north of peak 12,187, a summit ahead which has saddles on both sides of it. The saddle to the south, without the power line, is Ophir Pass. Down the other side is the mountain gulch which surrounds the town of Ophir, but under no circumstances should you attempt to ski there. The jeep road on the Ophir side traverses down a very steep slope where the avalanche danger is extreme. Turn around at the top of the pass. The descent on the return is sure to be exciting, especially above treeline.

O

29

South Mineral Creek

Distance: 9 miles (14.4 kilometers)
Starting elevation: 9459 feet (2883 meters)
Elevation change: 360 feet (110 meters)
Rating: Novice
Time allowed: 6-7 hours
Avalanche danger: Moderate
Maps: 7.5' Silverton
7.5' Ophir

The South Mineral Creek Road is on the southern side of U.S. Highway 550 about 2 miles west of Silverton. It is virtually flat for the 4.5 miles to the South Mineral Campground, making for easy skiing, but the number of avalanche paths it crosses on the way make it important for skiers using this route to have some avalanche safety knowledge.

The ski route is in the runout zones of the slidepaths which it crosses. Skiers are not traversing a steep slope where their weight would initiate a slide, but they are exposed to danger from natural releases above. The route should not be skied when the Colorado Avalanche Information Center rates the avalanche danger for the southern mountains as high. The slidepaths presenting the greatest danger to skiers on the road here are southeast and south-facing, to the right of the road as you ski in. Slides from the north-facing slopes on the left can also reach the road at points farther in as the canyon narrows.

A mile from the highway, the road crosses a bridge. A mile beyond this, the slidepaths begin to reach the road. In these first 2 miles from the highway, avalanche danger is relatively low. A tour this far and back makes a pleasant 4-mile round-trip tour for novice skiers.

Some particularly big slidepaths reach the road just before and just after the jeep road to Clear Lake branches off to the right 3.7 miles from the highway. Beyond this, the road reaches the South Mineral Campground at 4.5 miles. This area is a wild spot deep in the mountains, with the creek running through the evergreen forest. The

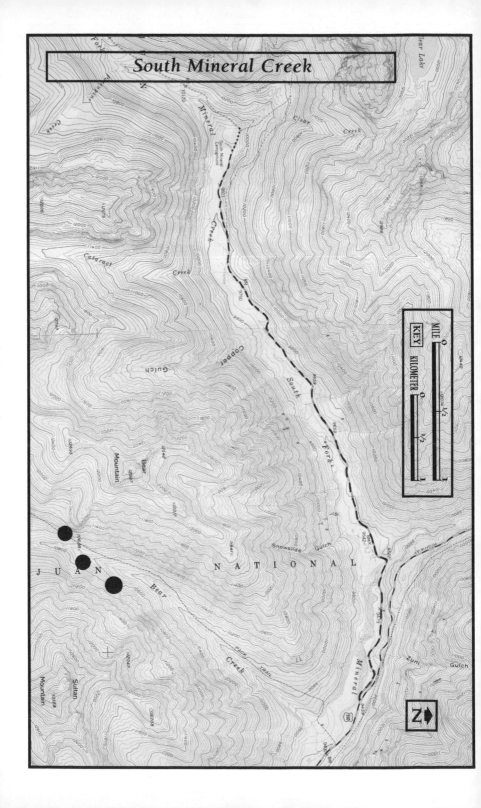

South Mineral Creek

campground is on the left of the road; continuing straight ahead a short distance brings you to a stream crossing where there is an interesting waterfall upstream on the right.

○

30

Minnie Gulch

Distance: 11-15 miles (18-24 kilometers)
Starting elevation: 9680 feet (2950 meters)
Elevation change: 1880-3080 feet
  (573-939 meters)
High points: 11,560-12,760 feet
  (3523-3889 meters)
Rating: Advanced
Time allowed: 6-8 hours
Avalanche danger: Moderate - High
Map: 7.5' Howardsville

From the northern end of Silverton, bear right on Colorado Highway 110 and drive 4 miles to Howardsville. The pavement ends at 2 miles. At Howardsville, the Cunningham Gulch Road bears right; your route — the road towards Eureka and Animas Forks — bears left. There should be room to park where plowing stops, just beyond the buildings of the Sultan Mountain Mine - P&G Mining.

For the next 2.5 miles, ski north up the road, which is flat on the valley floor. The runout zones of big slidepaths cross the road at 0.4, 0.7, and 1.3 miles from Howardsville. They present a hazard in times of high probability of natural releases. This route should not be skied when overall avalanche danger is high.

You pass an abandoned house with a saddle-shaped roof at 1.7 miles; this is the vicinity of Middleton, which once bustled with mining activity. Maggie Gulch is the valley to the right next, at 1.9 miles. Half a mile beyond this you will see the ruins of a structure which was probably part of the old mining tram shown on topo maps; no cable crosses the road any more. Watch to your right beyond this point for the Minnie Gulch jeep road. There is a sign, but it will be buried in the snowpack for much of the winter.

The Minnie Gulch Road goes into the timber to the right for a hundred yards, then makes a sharp left and traverses uphill. This is a primitive road, meaning steep. It rounds a couple of switchbacks and

Alpine tundra on the route to the Continental Divide.

traverses a south-facing slope high above the creek. There is a rough spot here where a rockslide has wiped out the roadbed. Further on, the road crosses the creek; a big slidepath coming down from the right here could reach the road, but you are not exposed to it for long. You pass the ruins of a mill on your left, and at a point 1.3 miles from the start of the Minnie Gulch Road, come to a rather substantial three-story abandoned building. Like all such structures, it could be dangerous to enter in its deteriorating state.

The road continues uphill to the right of the creek, then crosses it again. A bit beyond this, 0.4 mile beyond the buildings, a side road heads uphill to the left. The ski route stays to the right, with the creek farther to the right. One-quarter mile beyond the road junction, the route passes a one-room cabin.

In the next mile, the road continues to climb steadily. Several slidepaths cross it from steep west-facing slopes on the left; this is an area of high avalanche danger. The trees thin out here even between the slidepaths, and finally give up altogether as the route reaches the alpine tundra. The road is out of sight beneath the snowpack above treeline. The ski route stays to the left of the creek and continues traversing upward, heading a bit east of south.

The ruins of the Esmerelda Mine are atop a short steep pitch above treeline a mile from the one-room cabin; they will probably be mostly

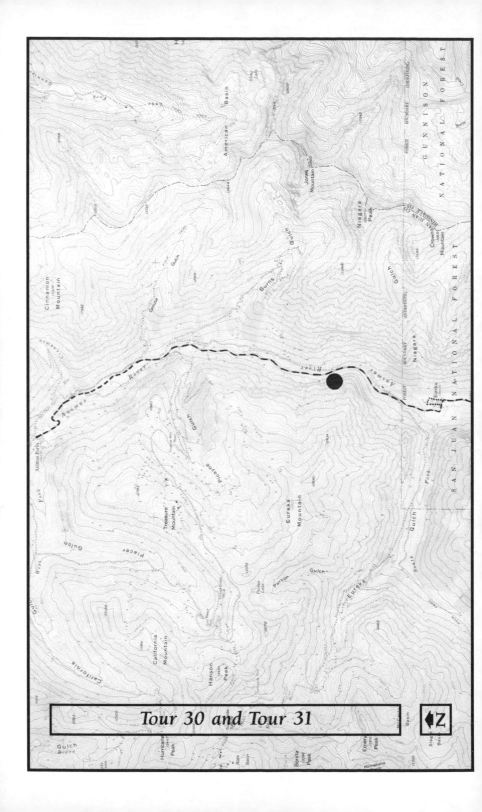

Tour 30 and Tour 31

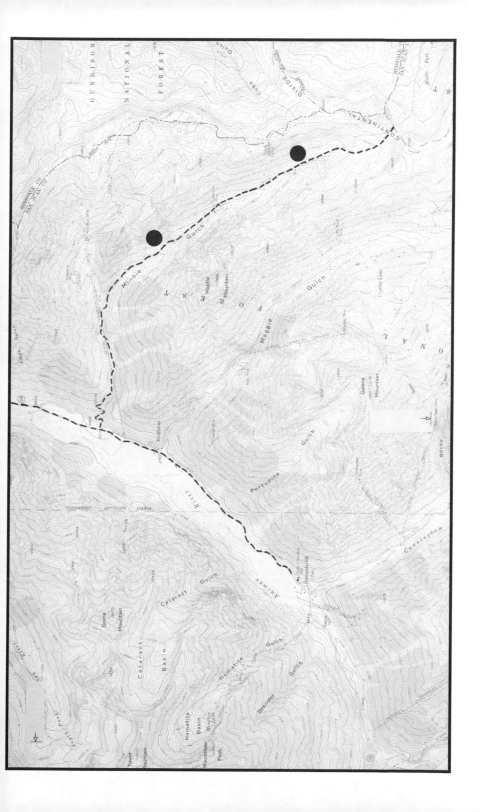

or completely buried in the snowpack. The steep pitch, though short, presents an avalanche hazard. This is the turnaround point for the shorter tour described in the heading.

From the Esmerelda Mine, it is an additional 2 miles and 1200 feet of ascent to the Continental Divide at the head of the gulch. The first section above the mine ruins is a cake walk at a gentle grade. It ends at a steep slope which must be ascended; be alert for avalanche danger here. At all times you need to stay well to the left of and above the creek gully.

Beyond the top of the steep slope, which will be a challenging drop on your descent, a more moderate grade leads you to the lip of a bowl. You have to descend slightly to cross it, then climb out the other side; the least-steep route up the other side is reasonably obvious, a bit to the right. Above the bowl, a moderately steep climb takes you the last half mile to the Divide.

The Great Divide here is a small pass at 12,760 feet elevation. The steep, brooding face of a rocky peak presides over it on the northeast. When I stood here, I felt a temptation to cast all caution aside and ski down the other side. I knew, though, that the descent back down Minnie Gulch — for which I would need all the energy I had left — would be exciting enough.

On the descent, stay well to the right of the creek gully below the bowl. Heading too far left could get you into trouble at a cliff band just above the creekbed. Skiing the creekbed is not a good idea; it puts you beneath slopes steep enough to avalanche on you in terrain where you are boxed in. Also watch out for the steep drop to the "cake walk;" you can come upon it suddenly from above and run into trouble with exposed rocks and avalanche potential.

The portion of this tour above treeline is good for spring skiing. At some time in April, the road from Howardsville may be plowed as far as Eureka, enabling you to drive to the Minnie Gulch trailhead. This cuts 5 flat miles from the round trip to the Divide. Snow conditions below treeline may be funky, and the south-facing section of road melts off fairly early. All cautions as to avalanche danger continue to apply in spring conditions, when wet slab slides occur in this area.   O

31

Eureka and Animas Forks

Distance: 8-16 miles (13-26 kilometers)
Starting elevation: 9680 feet (2950 meters)
Elevation change: 160-1520 feet (49-463 meters)
Rating: Novice - Intermediate
Time allowed: 4-8 hours
Avalanche danger: Moderate - High
Maps: 7.5' Howardsville
7.5' Handies Peak
San Juan County (topographic)
San Juan National Forest

In the summer, jeeps brings a steady stream of visitors up the rough road from Howardsville to the ghost towns of Eureka and Animas Forks; in the winter, the ghosts have the spectacular canyon of the upper reaches of the Animas River all to themselves. A ski tour as far as Eureka can be managed by novices. The trip to Animas Forks is a longer haul, 8 miles one way, and exposes the skier to greater avalanche danger.

From the northern end of Silverton, bear right on Colorado Highway 110 and drive 4 miles to Howardsville. The pavement ends at 2 miles. At Howardsville, the Cunningham Gulch Road bears right; your route – the road to Eureka and Animas Forks – bears left. There should be room to park where plowing stops, just beyond the buildings of the Sultan Mountain Mine - P&G Mining.

The 3.6 miles to Eureka are flat. Porcupine Gulch is to the right 1 mile in; an abandoned house with a saddle-shaped roof is on the left at 1.7 miles. This is the location of Middleton, which once bustled with mining activity. Maggie Gulch is on the right just ahead. The Minnie Gulch Trail goes off to the right in the evergreens 2.5 miles from Howardsville.

The runout zones of big slidepaths cross the road at 0.4, 0.7, and 1.3 miles from Howardsville. They present a hazard in times of high probability of natural releases. This route should not be skied when

Ski tracks on the route to Animas Forks.

overall avalanche danger is high. The valley here is broad enough that you can ski off to the left to give the avalanche runout areas some distance. The danger is worse beyond Eureka, where the route traverses steep slidepaths in their acceleration zones.

At Eureka, the terrain is open. The ruins of the Sunnyside Mill cling to the cliff to the west. To their left, the gorge of the South Fork of the Animas cuts deeply into the mountainside. To the north, much less obvious, a low log cabin lies buried in the snow. This is the turnaround point for novice skiers. All skiers should turn back from here in times of moderate or high avalanche danger. Ahead, the terrain gets steep and exposure to terrain with high avalanche danger potential is unavoidable. It is a 1360-foot climb to Animas Forks.

From Eureka, the road crosses the river and starts to climb,

heading north along the western wall of the Animas River Canyon. From here on, snowdrifts and avalanche debris obscure the roadway at many points. For 2 miles, the canyon is so narrow that you have little choice as to where to go in any case. The steep cliffs and rocky river gorge are as dangerous as they are spectacular; keep watch above for falling rocks as well as snowslide danger.

A mile from Eureka, the canyon broadens a bit. In another mile, it opens up still more. The road crosses the river in this area and follows the eastern wall of the canyon north from Grouse Gulch. It is not essential to stay on the road at this point, but stay on the right side of the valley to avoid a gorge which is between you and Animas Forks on the left. The town will come into view as you continue up the valley; it sits at an elevation of 11,200 feet.

As you reach the skeletal houses surrounded by a white wilderness, you might contemplate the fact that some miners wintered here when the place was active. In those days, a century ago, Thomas Walsh owned the big house with the bay window. He later made a fortune from the Camp Bird Mine near Ouray.

The return trip is a descent steep enough to take you back to Eureka in about half the time the ascent took. Only skiers with good downhill control should ski this route. The terrain is rough and moderately steep much of the way, especially rough if you have to traverse icy avalanche debris.

○

East from Durango to Pagosa Springs

Forest roads in the Pine Ranger District of the San Juan National Forest provide the opportunity for lakeside and forest skiing in terrain with little avalanche danger. Winter logging activity is possible on some forest roads; contact the Pine Ranger District Office in Bayfield, telephone 303 884-2512, for information.

O

32

Miller Creek (Lemon Lake)

Distance: 6 miles (9.6 kilometers)
Starting elevation: 8214 feet (2504 meters)
Elevation change: 1000 feet (305 meters)
Rating: Intermediate
Time allowed: 4-5 hours
Avalanche danger: Moderate
Maps: San Juan National Forest
7.5' Lemon Lake

Nature is reclaiming an abandoned forest road on the eastern shore of Lemon Lake. Pine and aspen trunks have fallen across the roadway; streams are cutting gullies in it. Years from now, the aspen saplings growing in parts of the old roadbed will completely wipe out all evidence of human intrusion. Until then, the forgotten road in winter will continue to provide a ski touring route which leads nowhere in particular. That just might be somewhere worth going.

To reach the road to nowhere, take Florida Road (La Plata County Road 240) from the intersection of East 3rd Avenue and 15th Street in Durango. After 13.7 miles, the paved road takes a sharp right and the dirt road to Lemon Lake (County Road 243) goes straight ahead. The Lemon Lake Road is messy in winter, likely to paint your car with red mud. Two-wheel drives can generally manage, as there are no steep grades.

In less than 2 miles from the start of the dirt road, Lemon Dam appears on the left. From here it is 1.6 miles to the start of the ski tour, which is visible as an unplowed road on the right. If you cross Miller Creek and see the plowed road to Sierra Verde Estates, you have gone too far. This plowed road is the one shown on the San Juan National Forest Map — the road for skiing is not shown. Miller Creek Campground, on the left side of the road, is also a little beyond the beginning of the ski route.

Parking on the side of the road is generally permissible. During or just after a snowstorm, however, the road should be kept clear

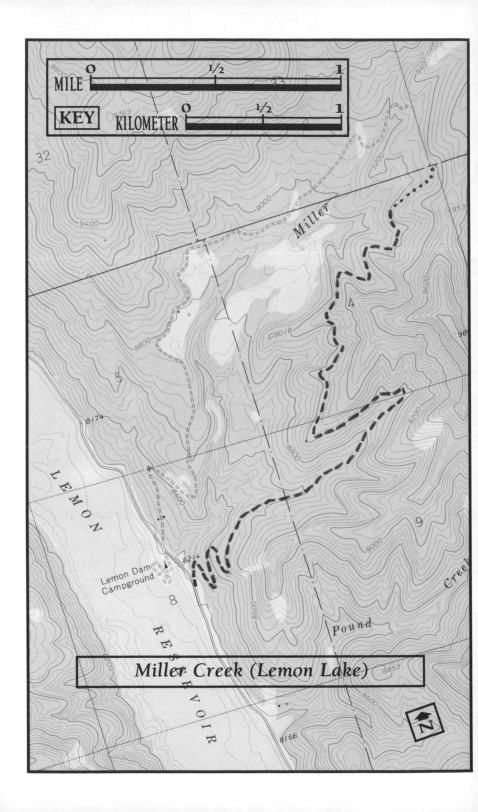

Miller Creek (Lemon Lake)

for plows.

Skiing begins beneath ponderosa pines. The road climbs steeply for the first mile, making four switchbacks up through the lakeside forest. If you stop for a moment on the third switchback, you should be able to hear Miller Creek — below and to the left — cascading down the slope. After the switchbacks, the road continues uphill at a gentler grade for about a mile to an aspen grove with a high cliff visible beyond. Watch the slope on your left here; this is where the road goes, making another switchback and climbing up and out of the drainage you have been ascending.

The ascent after the switchback leads you to a point with a view over the lake. A spur road branches off uphill to the right just before this; it is not the main route. From the viewpoint, the main route contours around the ridge. You turn away from the lake again and head for the hills.

More bumps in the trail — cross-country moguls? — mark snow-covered logs and irregularities. Crossings of stream gullies become more challenging, requiring side-stepping down one side and up the other. Even as the road grows wilder and woolier, however, civilization intrudes: houses in Sierra Verde Estates become visible to the left. Half a mile away and below, they interfere minimally with the forest experience.

Slopes steep enough to produce small avalanches exist in this area. Danger from them would exist only under extremely unstable snow-pack conditions, but cannot be ruled out entirely. However, in times when the avalanche danger below treeline is rated low, there is certainly no danger here.

At last the road peters out, at a point where the hillside it has been traversing cuts to the right. The time and mileage in the description at the beginning presume a turnaround at this point.

Skiers who wish to can explore further. Taking the turn to the right, down a short descent by a big evergreen, leads to an aspen-forested bowl with some openings and streambeds where telemarkers could make a few turns. Spending an hour in this wilderness setting is worth doing before heading back.

East from Durango to Pagosa Springs

Beyond this there is rough country with big, steep, treed-in ups and downs for many miles. The road has taken you only to the edge of nowhere.

O

33

Vallecito Lake Routes

It is 14 miles east on U.S. Highway 160 from Durango to Bayfield, where the Vallecito Lake Road heads north. It is then 14 miles to the southern end of the lake.

A
V A L L E C I T O   D A M   T O   P I N E   P O I N T

> *Distance:*   7.5 miles (12 kilometers)
> *Starting elevation:*   7765 feet (2367 meters)
> *Elevation change:*   95 feet (29 meters)
> *Rating:*   Beginner
> *Time allowed:*   4 hours
> *Avalanche danger:*   Low
> *Maps:*   La Plata County (topographic) Sheet 3
> 7.5' Vallecito Reservoir
> 7.5' Ludwig Mountain

At the southern end of Vallecito, just below the dam, La Plata County Road 501 forks to loop around the lake. The right fork takes you 0.3 mile up to the dam, which is crossed by the unplowed road. There should be room for parking at the roadside just before the dam; do not park on the dam itself.

Ski across the dam. The snow is exposed to wind and sun and gets rather crusty; this will be the trickiest section for first-time skiers. Snow conditions on the eastern shore of the lake where the road continues are better.

Following the lakeshore around to the northeast, you pass Old Timers Campground in a bit over a mile. In 2 more miles of easy skiing on the flat, you reach Graham Creek and North Canyon campgrounds. Half a mile beyond North Canyon, Pine Point Campground is your destination. On a sunny winter day, a lunch stop here before heading back will be a pleasant extension of your picnicking season.

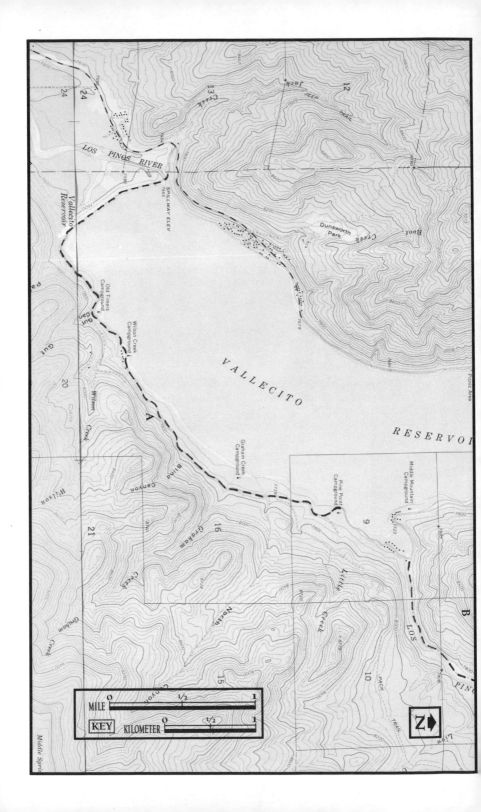

LOS PINOS RIVER

Vallecito Reservoir

SPILLWAY ELEV. 7665

Dunsworth Park

VALLECITO   RESERVOI

Old Timers Campground

Wilson Creek Campground

Graham Creek Campground

Pine Point Campground

Middle Mountain Campground

7723

Blind Canyon

Graham Creek

North Creek

Little Creek

7239

A

B

JEEP TRAIL

Pack Trail

Lion

Middle Spring

MILE   0   1/2   1
KEY   KILOMETER   0   1/2   1

N

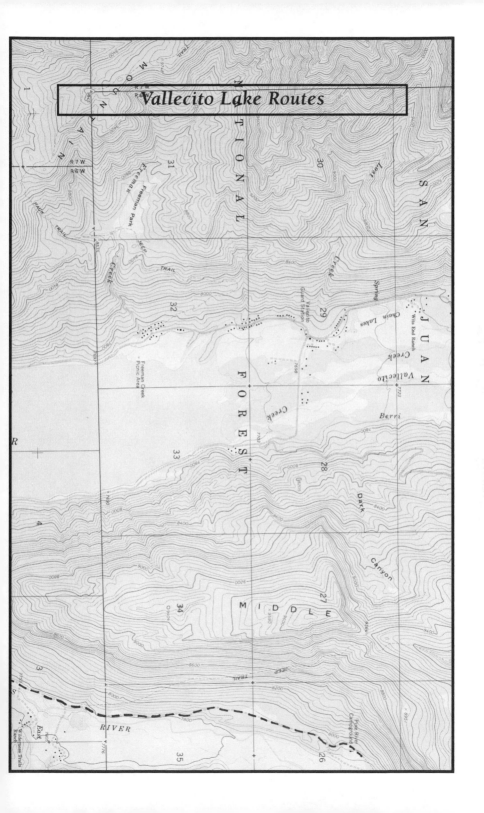
Vallecito Lake Routes

Pine River trailhead.
Tour 33-B

B

P   I   N   E   R   I   V   E   R

Distance: 6.5 miles (10.4 kilometers)
Starting elevation: 7720 feet (2353 meters)
Elevation change: 180 feet (55 meters)
Rating: Novice
Time allowed: 4 hours
Avalanche danger: Low
Map: 7.5' Vallecito Reservoir

The left fork of County Road 501 from the southern end of Vallecito follows the western shore of the lake, then goes around the northern end of the lake and heads south along the eastern shore. In 8.3 miles, snow plowing ends at the Elk Point Lodge. Park here, leaving room for snow plows to turn around.

The ski route leads you west, away from the lake, and then north, following the road which itself follows the Pine River. The grade varies from flat to moderately uphill. This is ponderosa pine country.

East from Durango to Pagosa Springs

You cross two cattle guards and reach the point where the road to Wilderness Trails and Teelawuket ranches branches off to the right. Much of the land on either side of the road all along this route is privately owned. Public access is limited to the road.

Beyond another cattle guard, a road to Penn and Granite Peaks ranches branches off to the right. Pine River Campground, a relatively primitive one, is not far ahead. Not far beyond it is the Pine River trailhead, the turnaround point for this tour. The Pine River Valley ahead looks like Yosemite; it gives you the feeling that you have really gotten somewhere.

O

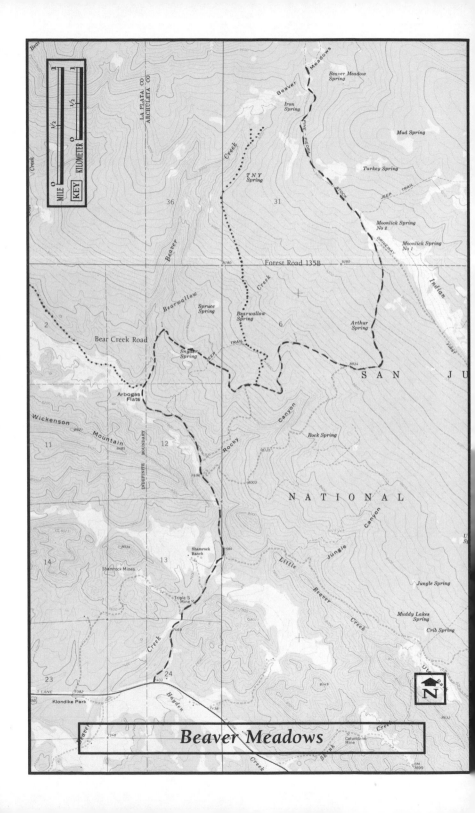

Beaver Meadows

34

Beaver Meadows

Distance: Up to 15 miles (24 kilometers)
Starting elevation: 7780 feet (2371 meters)
Elevation change: Up to 1820 feet (555 meters)
High point: 9600 feet (2926 meters)
Rating: Novice - Intermediate
Time allowed: Up to 8 hours
Avalanche danger: Low
Maps: 7.5' Baldy Mountain
San Juan National Forest 1985 Travel Map

The Beaver Meadows Road heads north from U.S. Highway 160 at a point 8 miles east of Bayfield. This is 22 miles east of Durango and 34 miles west of Pagosa Springs. The ski route description which follows assumes that you will be able to drive 2.2 miles up the Beaver Meadows Road and park at a gate which is closed in winter; four-wheel drive will help as the road may be muddy or snowpacked. On the way, stay right where a side road goes left. In times of heavy snow, you may have to park closer to the highway than this.

Beyond the gate, the road is flat for 0.75 mile, then begins a climb which lasts a long time. The Bear Creek Road branches off to the left at 1.3 miles. It makes a fine ski route with moderate climbing after the first short descent; novices should be able to handle it. A trip 2.5 miles along it to an open meadow which comes just after a bit of descent is a pleasant tour.

The Beaver Meadows Road continues climbing, entering higher-altitude forest where aspen and fir begin to mingle with the pines. At a point 2.8 miles from the gate, there is a view of the La Platas to the west. Not far beyond, at 3.2 miles, Forest Road 135B branches off uphill to the left.

Forest Road 135B makes a good intermediate tour. It becomes more primitive, climbs through attractive forests for 3 miles and dead ends after a brief descent. Skiing it to the end — where it forks, with both directions leading to dead-ends in a quarter mile — and then returning

The forest at trailside off Forest Road 135B.

gives you a 12-mile tour. A short distance up this side road, white fir trees are prominent in the forest, perfect Christmas trees when nature has decorated them with fresh snow.

The main Beaver Meadows Road ascends more gradually. Side roads branch off to the right at 4 and 4.4 miles from the gate. About 5.25 miles from the gate, the forest is a classic example of the fir-aspen type. Farther along, you cross a cattle guard and reach the high point of the tour, elevation 9600 feet, 6.7 miles from the gate.

From the high point, the route descends to the Beaver Meadows themselves. The open areas near the road are not large; a spruce-fir forest is dominant. In this cool, flat-bottomed valley between slopes which rise north to the San Juans, you can expect the snow to be deeper and more powdery than it was on the climb.

East from Durango to Pagosa Springs

The road crosses the flats and starts to climb again 8 miles from the gate. The 15-mile tour referred to in the heading assumes that you turn around before reaching that point, while still in the flat Beaver Meadows. The 1800 feet of descent on the return will help you return in your tracks in about half the time the ascent took. It is still a good long trek, an all-day excursion far into the woods which is free from avalanche danger.

○

Additional Area
East from Durango to Pagosa Springs

F O S S E T T G U L C H

The Fossett Gulch Road heads south from U.S. Highway 160 at a point 14.5 miles east of Bayfield. This is 28.5 miles east of Durango and 27.5 miles west of Pagosa Springs. It climbs a moderate grade for the first 2 miles, then starts descending. A good ski tour is possbile as far as the fourth cattle guard, 3.4 miles from the highway; somewhat beyond this, the road is plowed because of residences which it accesses from the other end. This route is primarily in ponderosa pine and is suitable for novice to intermediate skiers; there is no avalanche danger.

O

Pagosa Springs Area

A full range of ski touring, from easy forest strolls to challenging high backcountry telemarking, is available in the vicinity of Pagosa Springs and Wolf Creek Pass. Most tours listed here are in the Pagosa District of the San Juan National Forest; the office is in Pagosa Springs, telephone 303 264-2268. Areas east of the Continental Divide are in the Rio Grande National Forest District served by the Del Norte Office, telephone 303 657-3321, which includes the Wolf Creek downhill ski area.

One attraction of this area is following a ski tour with a dip in the hot mineral baths in town. The Spa Motel, telephone 303 264-5910, has 108-degree men's and women's indoor pools and a naturally-heated coed outdoor pool at a more moderate temperature. The Pagosa Springs Inn, telephone 303 264-2287, has an outdoor deck with four hot tubs of the natural hot springs water. Both are on Bridge Street and both charge $3 per hour for public use of the baths, which are also available to those who stay at the motels.

O

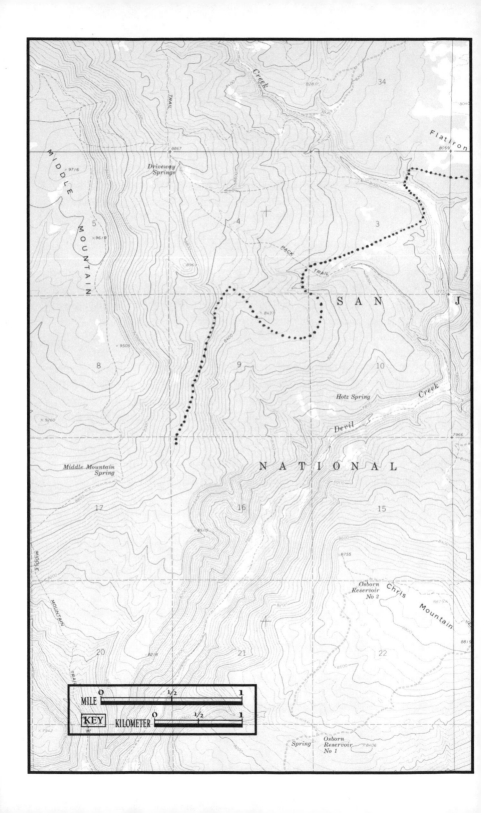

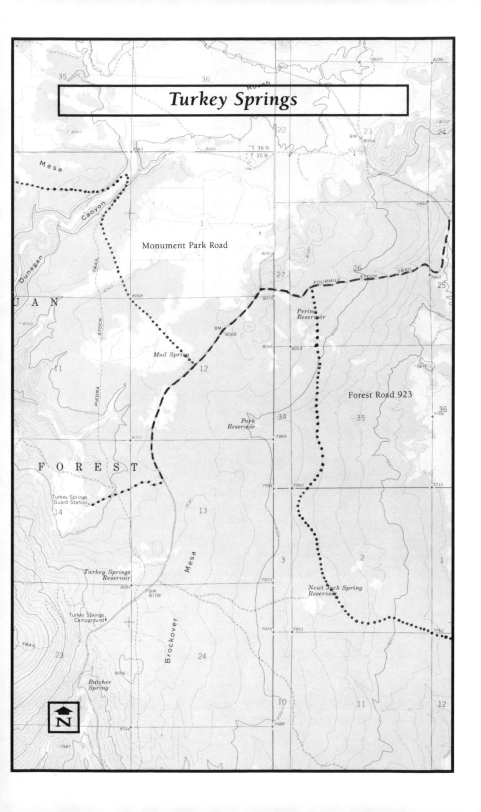

35

Turkey Springs

Distance: 6.8 miles (11 kilometers)
Starting elevation: 7840 feet (2390 meters)
Elevation change: 228 feet (69 meters)
High point: 8068 feet (2459 meters)
Rating: Novice
Time allowed: 4 hours
Avalanche danger: Low
Maps: 7.5' Chris Mountain
San Juan National Forest 1985 Travel Map

To reach the Turkey Springs Road, head north on the Piedra Road which intersects U.S. Highway 160 at the top of the hill 2.5 miles west of Pagosa Springs. It is 6.5 miles up the Piedra Road to the point where the Turkey Springs Road heads off to the left.

Skiing begins beyond the gate on the road, which is closed in winter. The route is uphill at a moderate grade for the first mile. Forest Road 923, a possible side trip, branches off to the left. Farther on, the road enters open pastures (after crossing a cattle guard) where it may be somewhat hard to follow; stay left rather than bearing right into the open fields. White arrows on small posts, marking the vehicle route in summer, also function as winter trail blazes. They are few and far between, however.

The pasture area is the high point of the road and affords the widest views. The ponderosa pine forest along much of the rest of the road is fairly open and inviting for some off-road exploring.

A little over 2 miles from the Piedra Road, the Monument Park Road branches off to the right. This road goes about 6 miles to a dead-end in the forest, crossing canyons after the first mile with more ups and downs than the Turkey Springs Road. Intermediate skiers can explore it as an alternate route. Continuing along the Turkey Springs Road, the forested high point of Chris Mountain (really just a hill by San Juan standards) can be seen ahead.

Descending slightly, the Turkey Springs Road reaches the turnoff to

*Stream near
Turkey Springs
guard station
in March.*

the Turkey Springs guard station 3.4 miles from the Piedra Road. This is the turnaround point for this tour. The branch road to the guard station is a half-mile side trip; there are no public facilities at the guard station itself which is closed and locked in the winter. On the trip back, as you return through the pasture area, Pagosa Peak can be seen in the distance beyond the pines.

○

36

Williams Creek Lake

Distance: 3-8 miles (5-13 kilometers)
Starting elevation: 8180 feet (2493 meters)
Elevation change: 150-200 feet (46-61 meters)
Rating: Beginner - Novice
Time allowed: 2-5 hours
Avalanche danger: Low
Maps: 7.5' Oakbrush Ridge
        7.5' Cimarrona Peak
        San Juan National Forest

The road to Williams Creek Lake, a reservoir on a tributary of the Piedra River, provides easy skiing in a very scenic area. It is reached by a 22-mile drive on the Piedra Road, which heads north from U.S. Highway 160 at the top of the hill 2.5 miles west of Pagosa Springs. The Williams Creek Lake Road is on the right; there should be room for parking at its intersection with the Piedra Road.

Soon after you start skiing, the side road to the Williams Creek Campground branches off to the right. The campground, occupied solely by old man winter during the snow season, makes a pleasant side trip. Continuing along the Williams Creek Lake Road, you pass some cabins on the right, climb slightly, and come into view of the lake.

The turnoff to the Teal Picnic Ground and fishing area is on the right a mile and a half from the Piedra Road. A couple hundred yards of skiing brings you to the lakeshore through scattered pines. The shorter distance and time given in the heading are for a tour this far and back.

Returning to the road, it is possible to continue skiing another 3.2 miles to the end of the road. It is easy skiing on flat terrain all the way. The Cimarrona Campground is 2.5 miles beyond the picnic ground; the longer distance and time given in the heading presume a trip this far.

○

Skiing into the Teal Picnic Ground.

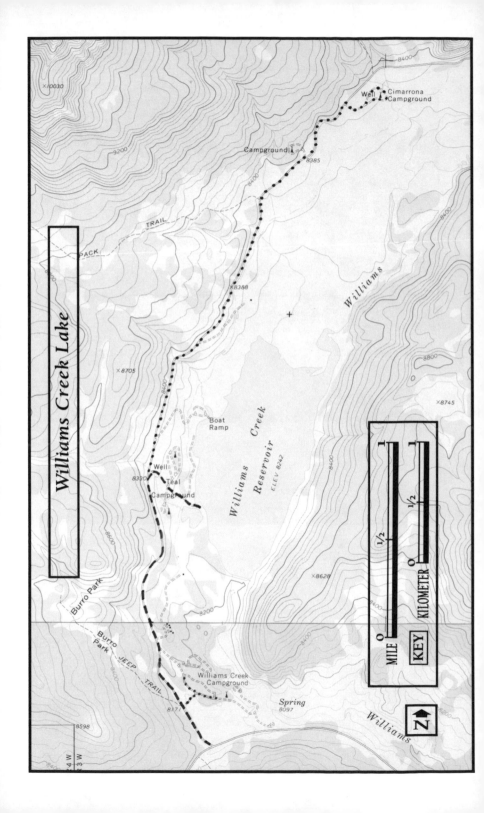

Williams Creek Lake

Williams

Williams Creek Reservoir
ELEV 8542

Cimarrona
Campground
Well

Campground
×8385

TRAIL

PACK

×8388

×8705

×10030

×9200

×8800

×8745

Boat
Ramp

Well
8300
Teal
Campground

×8628

Burro Park

Burro
Park

JEEP

TRAIL

Williams Creek
Campground

Spring
8097

Williams

8171

8598

4 W
3 W

KEY

MILE

KILOMETER

O   1/2   1

O   1/2   1

N

37

Pagosa Pines Touring Center

Post Office Box 4040
Pagosa Springs, Colorado 81157
303 731-4141 ext. 2021

Maintained tracks for beginner - intermediate skiers
Distance: 6-7.5 miles (10-12 kilometers)
Starting elevation: 7000 feet (2134 meters)
Trail fee: $4.50
Equipment rental: $8.50/day; $5/half day
(after 1 pm); $6.50/day for children under 12
Trail map: Available at touring center

This ski touring center at the Fairfield Pagosa resort is located on the rolling terrain of the golf course, which has good views to the peaks of the Continental Divide to the east. The center is located in the gray clubhouse building near a sign for the "Pagosa Pines Golf and Ski Touring Club." This is reached by entering the Fairfield Pagosa development on the access road called Pinion Causeway, just west of the lodge, 3 miles west of Pagosa Springs on U.S. Highway 160. Follow Pinion Causeway, then Carlee Place, to Pines Club Place where the clubhouse is on the right.

Cross-country skiing equipment is available for rental or purchase at the clubhouse. Instruction, including regularly scheduled group lessons, and guided backcountry tours are also available. The touring center is open from November 1st to the end of March, snow conditions permitting.

○

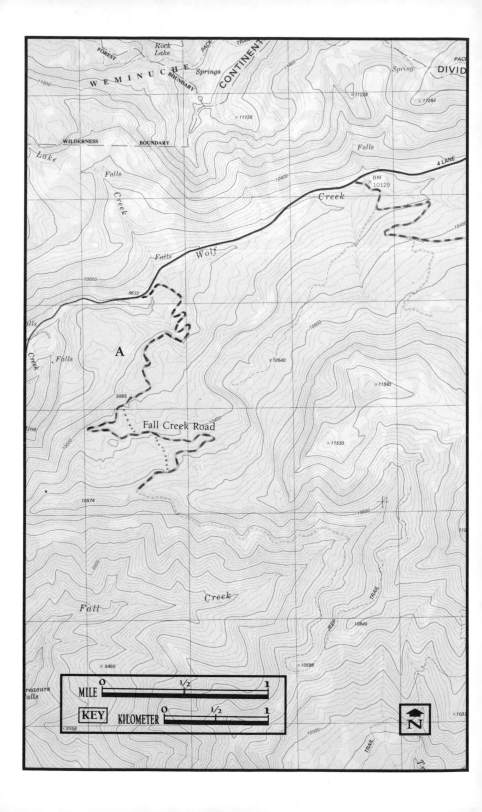

FOREST

Rock
Lake

PACK   TRAIL

Springs

CONTINENT-

DIVID

W E M I N U C H E

BOUNDARY

Spring

PAC

×11228

×11264

×11735

Lake

Falls

WILDERNESS   BOUNDARY

Falls

Creek

10400

Creek

Falls

4 LANE

×BM
10129

10400

Falls   Wolf

10000

9632

10600

A

×10540

×11563

9985

Fall Creek Road

10400

×11530

10574

10600

Falls

Creek

10000

9600

Fall   Creek

JEEP   TRAIL

10846

×9466

×10596

×1037

Treasure
Falls

| MILE | 0 | ½ | 1 |

KEY KILOMETER 0   ½   1

N

9358

10000

TRAIL

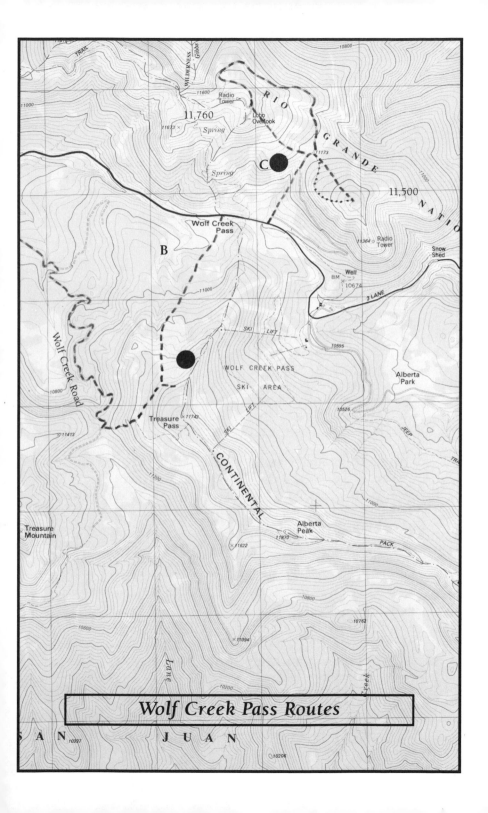

Wolf Creek Pass Routes

38

Wolf Creek Pass Routes

Skiers have ready access to the Continental Divide at Wolf Creek Pass, 23 miles east of Pagosa Springs on U.S. Highway 160. This area has the highest annual precipitation in Colorado, which translates into an abundance of powder snow in winter.

A

F A L L   C R E E K   R O A D

> **Distance:** 7 miles (11 kilometers) round trip
> **Starting elevation:** 9632 feet (2936 meters)
> **Elevation change:** 800 feet (244 meters)
> **High point:** 10,440 feet (3182 meters)
> **Rating:** Intermediate
> **Time allowed:** 4 hours
> **Avalanche danger:** Low
> **Map:** 7.5' Wolf Creek Pass

The Fall Creek Road is on the southern side of U.S. Highway 160 at a point 19.5 miles east of Pagosa Springs (3.5 miles west of the summit of Wolf Creek Pass). There is usually adequate parking space here, but this may not be the case during or just after big snowstorms. The sign for the road may be partially concealed by snowbanks.

The road drops briefly at the beginning and crosses a creek, then begins to climb. It rises steadily for the 3.5 miles of this tour, rounding many switchbacks. The beauty of this road as a ski route is that the slopes between the switchbacks are fairly open, permitting some shortcuts which telemarkers will find quite interesting on the descent. Non-telemarkers have a pleasant trip back down the road, which has a grade sufficient for a lot of gliding in medium to fast snow conditions.

This area is close enough to Wolf Creek Pass to partake of the magic of its powder. The first few miles of the road are not in avalanche

198

terrain, but it gets into rougher country farther along when it enters the gulch of Fall Creek. The turnaround point for this tour is before the road enters the gulch, where slopes on the hillside to the left are steep enough to present avalanche danger.

The boreal forest along the route is attractive. The whitish trunks of corkbark fir, a variety of subalpine fir, are prominent in the woods as you climb. Natural beauty on an even greater scale is evident in the views of cliffs and snowy peaks which open up as you climb. Pine siskins may be chirping and flying about in the trees; seed-eating birds are active in the coniferous forest in winter.

B

SUMMIT TO WOLF CREEK ROAD

> *Distance:*   4.3 miles (7 kilometers) one way
> *Starting elevation:*   10,857 feet (3310 meters)
> *Elevation change:*   Up 743 feet (226 meters),
>   down 1470 feet (448 meters)
> *High point:*   11,600 feet (3536 meters)
> *Rating:*   Intermediate - Advanced
> *Time allowed:*   5 hours
> *Avalanche danger:*   Moderate - High
> *Map:*   7.5' Wolf Creek Pass

From the summit of the pass, this backcountry route heads south and stays west of the Continental Divide. You end up at the point where the Wolf Creek Road intersects U.S. Highway 160 from the south, 2 miles west and 728 feet below the summit.

From the Continental Divide sign at the summit, you can see the top of a big, open bowl to the south and slightly to your right. Pick a route through the boreal forest towards this. The climb up the bowl .should be made up the right side; the steeper left side presents high avalanche danger. The terrain in the bowl is rough and the climb to the top, over 700 feet above the pass, is a good piece of work.

From the top of the bowl (about 11,600 feet), traverse down, continuing to the south and west. You need to find a route to the saddle between the ridge of the Continental Divide which is on your left and Treasure Mountain which is on your right. Cliffs below you form an obstacle. There is an area where you can avoid cliffs and descend through narrow lanes between the trees on steep slopes; this is challenging skiing. The Treasure Mountain Trail (shown on topo maps) is in this area but is not blazed and is very obscure in winter.

At the saddle you are on the Wolf Creek Road, which is clear at some points but obscure beneath the snowpack at others. Descend following the road to the west. It stays above and to the right of the creek. There are some steep slopes on the way down, open enough to make for good skiing. From the saddle, it is about 2.5 miles back to the highway. The Wolf Creek Road crosses the creek about half a mile before reaching the highway. You should avoid the creek gully where it is deep and steep-walled; cornices on the banks could trigger small but dangerous avalanches.

C

PEAKS 11,760 AND 11,500

Distance: 4 miles (6.4 kilometers)
Starting elevation: 10,850 feet (3307 meters)
Elevation change: 1210 feet (369 meters)
Rating: Intermediate - Advanced
Time allowed: 4 hours
Avalanche danger: Moderate
Map: 7.5' Wolf Creek Pass

To the north of the summit of the pass, these two peaks offer high-altitude telemarking terrain which is easily accessible. Intermediate non-telemarkers can tour to the top of peak 11,760 for the view and

Peak 11,500 from Peak 11,760.
Tour 38-C

traverse or follow the route of an access road down.

The route begins in a clearing on the northern side of the highway 0.25 mile east of the summit of the pass. There is a snow depth gauge here. From this point, a steep cliff face high on peak 11,760 is visible to the left; it is somewhat below the actual top and well away from where you ski.

Rio Grande National Forest Road 402 begins here. It is marked with reflectors on posts which will be visible in all but the deepest snow. This road heads east, then makes a big switchback up through the woods to the saddle between peaks 11,760 and 11,500. It makes for a gentler but much longer ascent to the saddle than the route used by most skiers.

The skiers' route heads north, following an open lane through the timber on the eastern (right) side of the stream gully which you see from the clearing. Stay away from the left bank of the stream gully; it leads to a steep slope which can present high avalanche danger. The grade up the right bank is moderately steep. In a slow half mile — hard work because of the climbing — you reach the saddle; Forest Road 402 comes in from the right. A power line comes into view ahead.

From this point, follow Forest Road 402 to the top of peak 11,760. The road heads north, crosses under the power line, swings around to the west and traverses up the "back side" of the peak at a moderate grade. The distance from the saddle is about a mile. Snowmobiles are used on this route both for fun and for access to the radio towers on top of 11,760. These towers are an unmistakable landmark.

Atop peak 11,760, you are at treeline on the Continental Divide. This is 910 feet above Wolf Creek Pass. Views are wide and the wind may be fierce. The telemarking route descends the eastern face of the peak back to the saddle; the drop to the saddle is 560 feet in about half a mile. Head for the rounded summit of peak 11,500 which you can see to the east below you, a mile away as the raven flies. You can see routes up peak 11,500 from here.

As you start down to the saddle, there is a short very steep pitch to watch out for; it will challenge advanced skiers. Intermediate skiers traversing around this slope shold be aware of going too far to the right (south), where the cliffs and the steep slope present avalanche danger. They are avoidable.

The rest of the descent to the saddle is on a grade ideal for tele-markers of all ability levels. Snowmobiles mess up the snow in a big clearing just below the steep spot, but other openings in the forest just to the right provide open lanes which frequently have unbroken snow.

From the saddle, head east up peak 11,500. It is a 300-foot ascent to the top. If you bear to the right as you climb, you can get into the open area which you viewed from peak 11,760. On the descent, you can ski down this opening for a bit, but should bear right back towards the saddle before the clearing leads you down into very thick timber on very steep slopes. The downhill drop back to the pass is 650 feet.

These peaks are a veritable two-ring circus for telemarkers. Since distances are short, you can readily get in more than one run on each peak in a day of skiing. Conditions can be good for spring skiing here into mid-May. With a dawn start, you can often walk right up 11,760, ski its east slope when the snow first softens in the sun, and then take a run on 11,500 where the snow will not soften up until later due to a more westerly exposure. ○

Additional Areas
Pagosa Springs Area

Mileages to these forest roads are measured from the stoplight at Bridge Street in Pagosa Springs. The Pagosa Ranger District Office at 180 Pagosa Street is a good place to check on the current status of these roads; the East Fork in particular may be affected by downhill ski development. The Tucker Ponds Trail is under the jurisdiction of the Del Norte Office of the Rio Grande National Forest.

M I L L   C R E E K   R O A D

Take the right onto Highway 64 south towards Chama 0.9 mile east of town. The Mill Creek Road is then a quick left. It will probably be plowed as far in as the last access point to private land. About 6 miles in, a side road heading uphill to the right makes a good intermediate ski route. It climbs and heads off towards Squaretop Mountain. Snowmobile use in this area is heavy.

F A W N   G U L C H   R O A D

This road is on the southern side of Highway 160 at a point 4.4 miles east of town. It will probably be plowed as far in as the access point to a ranch; it can be skied beyond this point.

E A S T F O R K

This road is on the southern side of Highway 160 just after a bridge over the East Fork of the San Juan River, 10.5 miles east of town. It is not plowed; park at the road side. The road crosses an open field (private land) and enters the national forest at the East Fork Campground.

The way is mostly flat with a few gentle hills which novice skiers can handle. It is possible to ski a long way on this scenic route; 7 miles from the highway the route comes into the open at private land which may be developed as the East Fork Ski Area. The East Fork development proposal includes a center for Nordic skiing.

W E S T F O R K

This road is on the northern side of Highway 160 just before it begins to climb to Wolf Creek Pass, 14.5 miles east of town. A ski tour 4 miles in from the highway stays on flat terrain suitable for beginners.

Beyond this point, a pack trail continues into the Weminuche Wilderness (passing through private property on Borns Lake Ranch). The pack trail reaches Rainbow Hot Springs in 4 more miles which are very difficult on skis. The springs are hard to find and only moderately warm. Very strong and adventurous intermediate or better skiers, especially if they plan on winter camping, may want to attempt the trip.

Ice fall along the East Fork Road.

T U C K E R   P O N D S   T R A I L

Heading east from the summit of Wolf Creek Pass, you reach the upper end of this trail, which is on the right-hand side of Highway 160, less than a mile beyond the snowshed. This point is marked by a cross-country skier symbol. The other end of the trail is at the junction of Highway 160 and Pass Creek Road about 4 more miles down the highway. To ski it as a round trip, starting from the lower end will give you the climb first and the descent on the return for a total tour of 9 miles. Avalanche danger may exist on the first half mile of trail from the lower end; the route requires at least intermediate skiing ability.

Index

I

O

Ophir, 135
Ophir Pass, 136, 159
Ouray County Cross-Country Skiing Guide, 156

Ouray Hot Springs Pool, 140
Owl Creek Pass, 155

P

Pagosa Pines Touring Center, 195
Pagosa Springs Hot Springs, 187
Peaks 11,760 and 11,500, 200
Perins Peak State Wildlife Area, 37

Power Line Run (Coalbank Pass), 99
Purgatory Ski Touring Center, 83

R

Railroad Road, 56
Red Mountain Pass, 147
Rico, 125

Ridgway, 140, 144
Rio Grande National Forest, 187
Roaring Forks Road, 139

S

St. Paul Ski Lodge, 152
San Juan National Forest —
    Animas Ranger District, 71
    Dolores Ranger District, 110
    Mancos Ranger District, 47
    Pagosa Ranger District, 187
    Pine Ranger District, 172

Scotch Creek, 125
Silverton, 71
Silverton Avalanche School, 71
South Mineral Creek, 161
Spud Mountain Ridge, 101
Stoner Lodge, 139

I

T

U

V

W

O

The author on peak 11,500 in the Wolf Creek Pass area.

About the Author

Tom Lepisto, who now lives in Durango, began his backcountry skiing in New England. Since moving to Colorado he has continued to pursue his long-standing interests in hiking, wilderness areas, and the natural environment as well as skiing. He works as a freelance photographer and writer.

○